CONTENTS

PREFACE

The subject of "global interdependence" has become a frequent topic of reports and discussions among journalists, commentators, politicians and scholars in recent years. Indeed, there appears to be an increasing awareness among these opinion leaders—and the people in general—about the phenomena of global interdependence which envelop us in every aspect of our lives, from international trade to development assistance, from armed conflicts to clashes of cultures, and from tastes and life-styles to environmental problems. While such an awareness is encouraging, there appears to be a critical gap in the current debate about global interdependence when it comes to developing a systematic analysis of what global interdependence means for individuals and societies entangled in the network of complex connections and linkages with other individuals and societies.

This work represents one effort to fill this gap and attempts to develop a systematic analysis of the question of what global interdependence means for the individual and society. Analyzing this question is important for the individual because the task of establishing autonomy and identity for each individual has become quite an undertaking as the space of human development has dramatically expanded, thanks to the development of transportation and communications technologies. The question is also important for society not only because it, too, must concern itself with the issues of autonomy and identity but also because it is confronted with the enormous challenge of maintaining coherence and viability as a system amidst unpredictable forces of change over which it has little control.

Throughout the book concepts, ideas and theories from a variety of social and systems sciences will be employed to analyze the nature and implications of *INTERDEPENDENCE AND CHANGE IN THE GLOBAL SYSTEM.* A multi-disciplinary approach is essential in dealing with this subject because the world, as we see it, is an interdependent system among individuals, groups, organizations, communities, nations and nation-states, interacting with one another in a complicated web of actions, reactions, and repercussions. Since the subject we deal with is a complicated one, the book will tread over many terrains—history of science, epistemology, aesthetics, human development, economic development, political philosophy, social ethics, international relations, and global education. The main point of our analysis is that all these things are indeed related to one another in the world of global interdependence.

The book is thematically divided into six parts. Our journey into the world of global interdependence begins in part one with a review of the history of science. While the rational and reductionistic approach to knowledge acquisition as originated by Descartes has dramatically expanded the body of our knowledge of the world around us, that body of knowledge lacked coherence and unity until the emergence of systems approach in this century. Interpreted in the context of human development, what started out as the rational and reductionistic approach of Western science is now compatible with the intuitive and holistic tradition of the Eastern approach to knowledge acquisition. Part two examines how societies go about reconciling individual autonomy on the one hand and social order on the other. While every society is a cybernetic system in the sense that some degree of steering and control is involved, the influence the government has over the course of societal evolution gets diluted in liberal democratic societies as they are subject to several types of dysfunctions. Maintaining coherence amidst unpredictable forces of change, of which some originate in other societies, is an important challenge faced by every society. Part three examines this problem in the context of society's commitment to economic, technological and political development. Part four analyzes how the forces of social change, in the world of global interdependence, undermine the sovereignty of nation-states, erode the effectiveness of domestic policies and regulations, and necessitate the transformation of human systems. Part five looks into the problem of coordination and harmonization of laws, policies and value systems among societies operating in the world of global interdependence. The need for coordination and harmonization arises because culture, economy and polity cannot escape the fundamental conflict among themselves as subsystems of social systems. The book's journey into the world of global interdependence concludes in part six where the discussion returns to the theme of human development. While laws, policies and value systems can be coordinated and harmonized, the ultimate burden of maintaining coherence and viability of the world as a system falls on the individual who must cultivate consciousness about the necessity of reconciling the two realities of human existence—man as an individual and man as a species.

Tetsunori Koizumi
The Ohio State University
Columbus, Ohio

ACKNOWLEDGEMENTS

I would like to acknowledge Professor George E. Lasker of University of Windsor for his graciousness in allowing me to explore and present most of the ideas developed in this book at the Conferences and Symposia of the International Institute for Advanced Studies in Systems Research and Cybernetics of which he is President. Professor Jean Ramaekers, President of the International Association for Cybernetics, is also acknowledged for allowing me to test out some of the ideas discussed here at the International Congress of Cybernetics which he organizes. Organizers of the International Conference on Cultural Economics, the Big Ten Body of Knowledge Symposium, the Seminar on Autonomy and Interdependence, the World Congress of Philosophy of Law and Social Philosophy, and the European Meeting of Cybernetics and Systems Research are also acknowledged for allowing me to present preliminary versions of the papers which are included in this book.

During the final stage of preparing the manuscript, I have benefited from the able editorial assistance of Kei Koizumi who, as a student in international political economy, shares his father's interest in the issues discussed in this book. My long-time friend, Dr. Jon Cunnyngham, has performed a small miracle in transforming the manuscript into a final product with an aesthetic appeal which is rare among scholarly works of this sort. I must also extend my special acknowledgments to my wife, Hisako, who has provided me constant support and encouragement while I have been struggling with the issues dealt with in this book. While her name does not appear as co-author of this work, as it does in some recent works on which we collaborated, her influence is ubiquitous. To her constant support and encouragement this work is dedicated.

PART ONE

KNOWLEDGE ACQUISITION AND
HUMAN DEVELOPMENT

1. THE MODE OF THEORIZING AND THE NATURE OF KNOWLEDGE

Introduction

"If the doors of perception were cleansed every thing would appear to man as it is, infinite," writes William Blake in his work *The Marriage of Heaven and Hell*. In every society there are admittedly some individuals, like Blake, who are blessed with extraordinary powers of perception. As far as these extraordinary individuals are concerned, to perceive is to know, for reality is directly made comprehensible to their perception.

What about other individuals who, with their ordinary powers of perception, see reality only "through narrow chinks of their caverns"? Making sense of reality, to them, would involve deciphering of the shadows, as the celebrated Platonic metaphor has it, reflected on the walls of their caverns. Or, as Piaget explains in his *Genetic Epistemology*, "to know is to transform reality in order to understand how a certain state is brought about" (Piaget [1970], p.15). For ordinary individuals blessed only with ordinary powers of perception, acquiring knowledge of reality would thus require that some action be taken on their part.

Knowledge acquisition is, needless to say, one type of human action. A meaningful discussion of the nature of our knowledge of the world around us must therefore be conducted in the context of a theory of human action. This is what we propose to do in this chapter. As it will turn out, the nature of our knowledge of the world around us very much depends on the way we go about theorizing about reality.

Reality, Perception and Action

Abstracted from concrete situations, human action can be seen as going through two phases which may be termed "perceiving" and "acting". The "perceiving" phase of human action involves a mapping, f, which maps an element of reality space, X, into a perceptive image of that element in perception space, Y. In mathematical symbolism, this can be represented by $f:X \to Y$. The "acting" phase of human action, on the other hand, involves a mapping, g, which maps a perceptive image formed in perception space into a specific human action in action space, Z. That is, $g:Y \to Z$. Our conception of human action linking reality to perception to action can thus be represented by a composite mapping, h, of f and g as $h = g \cdot f: X \to Z$.

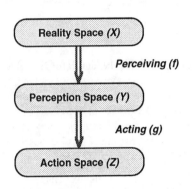

While human action can be represented as a composite of "perceiving" and "acting", there is no natural interpretation we can give to reality space, perception space and action space which would establish a unique relationship among them. The absence of uniqueness here is rather important. To illustrate this point, consider, for example, the case of human thought. Does thought represent a perception and, therefore, belong to perception space, or is it an example of human action which belongs to action space?

Thought can be considered as belonging to perception space, to the extent that it corresponds to a perceptive image of a particular thing or an event which, in turn, leads to some concrete action. But it is also possible to regard thought as belonging to action space, as Konrad Lorenz suggests in his *Behind the Mirror*: "All human thought can be seen as 'action' in a 'visualized' space...taking place within the nervous system" (Lorenz [1977], p.163). Here perception space is identified with the central nervous system housed in the brain, and action space with some abstract space representing the actions of the nervous system. There is, however, no compelling reason why we have to adopt this particular interpretation. In fact, the main purpose of our inquiry is to show how different interpretations of reality, perception and action spaces correspond to different modes of theorizing about reality and, therefore, lead to different forms of knowledge of the world around us. We shall therefore treat reality, perception and action spaces as reference sets for the two mappings of perceiving and acting.

Before we proceed to show how our analytical framework can be employed to analyze the nature of knowledge as implied by a specific mode of theorizing about reality, we introduce two specific terms. First, the image of a reality under the mapping called "perceiving", i.e., $f(X_i)$, where X_i is an arbitrary subset of reality space X, will be termed a "sense of reality". Thus, a "sense of reality" is a perceptive image of a reality formed within perception space, i.e., $f(X_i) \subset Y$. Second, the image of a perception under the mapping called "acting", i.e., $g[f(X_i)] = h(X_i)$, will be termed a "model of reality", which is a subset of action space, i.e., $h(X_i) \subset Z$.

Our use of the term "model of reality" is consistent with the scientist's use of the same term for a formal representation of reality. It is to be noted, however, that there is nothing in our conception of human action that would prevent us from using a "model of reality" to refer to a work of art. Although a work of art may lack precision as a representation of reality and, therefore, may not quite play the same role as a scientific model in guiding human action, it is nevertheless a meaningful, symbolic representation of reality produced by a particular type of human action.

The Cartesian Mode

Our discussion of "the mode of theorizing and the nature of knowledge" begins with Descartes' contribution, for it was Descartes who was most responsible for ushering in the age of democracy in knowledge acquisition. Descartes set down four rules which he regarded as essential to the success of his "method". Of the four the second rule deserves special attention for its simple message: "[D]ivide up each of the difficulties...into as many parts as possible...in order that it might be resolved in the best manner possible" (Descartes [1952], p.47). This rule has often been used as a justification for an arbitrary partitioning of reality space into non-intersecting component parts. Formally stated, this characteristic of the Cartesian mode means that reality space can be expressed as an arbitrary union of non-intersecting subsets, i.e., $X = \cup X_i$ with $X_i \cap X_j = \phi$.

The second characteristic of the Cartesian mode concerns the relationship between perception space and action space. The Cartesian mode relies exclusively on the power of reason as a guide to knowledge acquisition. As Descartes himself put it as the subtitle of his "method", his was a discourse on the "method of properly conducting one's reason and of seeking the truth in the sciences". Our sensory perception, on the other hand, is rejected as being unreliable in our search for knowledge of the world around us. Knowledge acquisition, to the Cartesians, is an exclusive activity of the mind which takes place in action space. Moreover, action space has no linkage to perception space when perception space is identified with the set of all sensory perceptions of the body. This does not mean that perception space is empty. To the extent that the body constitutes an object of knowledge, we have $Y \subset X$. And the Cartesian dualism between mind and body can be expressed as $Y \cap Z = \phi$. We thus have a simple mapping $h: X \rightarrow Z$ under the Cartesian mode of theorizing about reality, where h does not have to go through the two mappings of perceiving, f, and acting, g.

The Cartesian dualism between mind and body leads us to the third characteristic of the Cartesian mode of theorizing about reality. Not only is the act of theorizing, belonging as it does to action space, unrelated to perception space but it is also independent of reality space. This is so because senses of reality formed in perception space, instead of becoming raw data for models of reality, are never transmitted to action space. Formally speaking, we have $h(X) \cap X = \phi$. This implies that there is no interaction between objects of knowledge, which lie in reality space, and those who seek knowledge, whose actions lie entirely in action space. Such non-interaction is indeed the basis of a belief in the objectivity of science in which the scientist is viewed as a neutral observer of reality whose actions have no influence on the reality which he studies.

The three characteristics of the Cartesian mode of theorizing about reality have corresponding implications for the nature of our knowledge of the world around us. An arbitrary partitioning of reality space by the Cartesians implies that knowledge, to them, is something that can be divided and compartmentalized. Hence, knowledge can be acquired by specialists pursuing their own interests. In its extreme form, the Cartesian segmentation of reality space, granting these specialists intellectual property rights over their domains of specialty, has turned scientific inquiry into somewhat of a neurotic endeavor with their own conceptions of what constitutes reality space for their scientific disciplines.

The Cartesian veneration of the power of reason has left its mark on modern education in the form of a dichotomy between academic and non-academic subjects. While academic subjects, having to do with the activities of the mind, are cherished, non-academic subjects such as physical education and the arts, having to do with the activities of the body, are relegated to secondary roles in learning and human development.

The absence of interaction between objects of knowledge and those who seek knowledge has an equally disturbing implication. The "objectification" of reality enables the scientist to treat an object of his inquiry with a certain degree of detachment. Since the act of knowing about reality can be taken to be independent of reality itself, the scientist's knowledge of reality can be used to change reality—manipulate and control the environment—without fear of repercussion.

The Darwinian Mode

The Darwinian mode of theorizing about reality stands in sharp contrast to the Cartesian mode as a method of obtaining knowledge of the world around us. For one thing, reality space, under the Darwinian mode, cannot be partitioned arbitrarily into non-interacting component parts. This is so because reality space, as our natural environment, has its own history which has been shaped by a history of complicated and constantly changing patterns of ecological interaction among its constituent elements. As such, an event in reality space, like the emergence of a new species, cannot be explained by a simple cause-effect relationship which is observed in a particular segment of reality space. As Darwin himself states in Introduction to his *Origin of Species*, an event such as the origin of a species can be made comprehensible to us only "by patiently accumulating and reflecting on all sorts of facts which could have any bearing on it" (Darwin [1979], p.46).

The question regarding the emergence of a new species points to another characteristic of the Darwinian mode of theorizing about reality. The phenomenon of life, unlike the movement of a celestial body, does not follow a deterministic path which can be expressed in terms of, say, a differential equation with an arbitrary initial condition. The initial condition does matter as do all the subsequent conditions, for each species follows its own unique life history in relation to its constantly changing environment. Indeed, it is always a change at the margin, a deviation from the normal course of events, that holds a key to our understanding of the phenomenon of life. As a method of obtaining knowledge of the world around us, the Darwinian mode thus urges us to be on the lookout for an outlier in the distribution, for a variation in the normal pattern of interaction, and for a new phenomenon in the offing.

If each species has evolved with its own unique life history in relation to its constantly changing environment, it would follow that man as a species has also evolved in the same manner. That is, if we carry the Darwinian mode of theorizing about reality to where it logically leads us, there is no avoiding the conclusion that the descent of man as a species is also a part of natural history. To the Darwinians, therefore, all that we do as human beings must also be a part of the whole scheme of natural history, that is, $Z \subset X$.

If man as a biological being is no exception to the Darwinian mode, what about man as a spiritual being, as a species endowed with intellect? Is human intellect an exception to the laws of evolution? Again, to the Darwinians, there can be no room for doubt, though we had none other than Alfred Russell Wallace dissenting from Darwin on this question. The Darwinian mode of theorizing about reality is a self-contained scheme in the sense that the minds of those who seek knowledge of reality are also part of the same reality. This is in sharp contrast to the Cartesian mode in which the mind is seen as capable of leading a separate existence from the body and can, therefore, be outside the course of natural history. To the Cartesians, to know is to recall from a book of memory which exists independently of the physical body. To the Darwinians, however, knowing about reality must itself be a product of human evolution, for it is surely by knowing about reality that humans have learned how to adapt ourselves to the constantly changing environment.

The Freudian Mode

Freud's contribution to the body of our knowledge of the world around us can be seen as an extension of the Darwinian mode of theorizing about reality into the realm of the human psyche. In fact, it was Darwin himself who expressed a wish, at the conclusion of his *Origin of Species*, that psychology would emerge as one of the many disciplines in support of his theory of evolution. By extending his thesis into many research fields, he hoped, "much light will be thrown on the origin of man and his history" (Darwin [1979], p. 222).

The Freudian mode of theorizing about reality as an extension of the Darwinian mode offers us a new insight into the nature of reality space. While the Darwinian mode conceives the continuity of life in biological terms, the Freudian mode does so in psychological terms. In other words, the descent of man fits into the grand scheme of natural history not only because man as a biological being has evolved out of a branch of the tree of life but also because man as a psychological being shares with other animal species the continuity of psychic life. As later studies have come to confirm, we humans are not free from our evolutionary past as psychological beings because the brain, as the seat of our psychic life, is itself an evolutionary product, containing the remnant of our animal past. The Freudian conception of the continuity of psychic life thus adds a new dimension to the Darwinian conception of reality space by suggesting that the space of possible patterns of ecological interaction may involve our psychological states as well.

There is another, and perhaps more illuminating, way of looking at the revolutionary significance of the Freudian mode of theorizing about reality. What the above argument suggests is that, if we are to accommodate the Freudian mode, it is necessary to redefine reality space to include the "psychic" universe as well as the "physical" universe. But it is also possible to single out the strategic importance of psychic life for us humans and rethink the way in which human action is linked to perception space. Consider, for example, the classic case of hysteria discussed by Freud in his *Five Lectures on Psycho-Analysis*: "[The patients] cannot get free of the past and for its sake they neglect what is real and immediate" (Freud [1977], p.17). Here human action may be guided by a model of reality, but the corresponding reality is not to be found in reality space containing the immediate events but rather in perception space containing all the fantasies, imaginations and memories.

The case of hysteria aside, there is indeed no reason why our models of reality should always represent events and things in reality space. To the extent that the human psyche is a product of human evolution, we may short-cut the full process of formulating models of reality and base our actions on imagined realities to be found in perception space. In fact, what Freud unveiled to us is the possibility that human action often stems from "psychic" reality rather than "real" reality. What is being said here may be restated in terms of our analytical framework as: $z \varepsilon Z$ implies that there exists a $y \varepsilon Y$ such that $z = g(y)$. Or, as Shakespeare realized a long time ago with his poetic perception, "we are such stuff as dreams are made on." Formally speaking, this property, combined with the definition of g, gives us $Z = g(Y)$. This linkage between perception space and reality space is indeed what the Freudian revolution was all about.

That human action can follow directly from psychic reality has an important implication for human evolution. The process of human evolution, especially cultural evolution, is dominated by the Lamarckian inheritance of acquired norms and values. These acquired norms and values, to the extent that the adherence to them becomes automatic, infiltrate into the psychic reality of the members of a human society. While the adherence to these norms and values is necessary for social order, it suggests one way in which we humans become slaves to our psychic past. Moreover, our psychic past can very easily be turned into a shelter which we seek from the pressures imposed on us by "the high standards of our civilization" (Freud [1930]). The Freudian mode of theorizing about reality thus views our psychic life as being caught in a double bind between our commitment to the rational ego development as a driving force behind our civilization and our bondage to the psychic past into which the irrational *id* pushes us partly as a shelter from the pressures of civilization. Freud's solution of this double bind was to introduce a transcendental entity which he termed "Super ego". This, too, is an interesting variation in the theory of human action. To the extent that our social consciousness emerges out of such superstructure which society imposes on us, it, too, becomes a part of our psychic reality which guides our actions.

The Freudian mode of theorizing about reality can be employed to evaluate the meaning of the Cartesian mode in the context of our theory of human action. The Cartesian mode, which relies solely on the power of reason, would be regarded under the Freudian mode as incomplete and partial in that reason, or the power of reasoning, constitutes only a part of the totality of our perceptive faculties which defines perception space. The Freudian mode thus recognizes how scientists can be influenced by a specific cultural environment and thereby develop a certain mental habit to see only those things in reality space which appeal to their customary mode of theorizing about reality. Whether in science or in other endeavors, we are too prone to develop psychological *a priori* either out of our bondage to the psychic past or by social conditioning in the use of our perceptions. What is particularly disturbing about the use of psychological *a priori* in science is that it can very easily be combined with an arbitrary segmentation of reality space, another characteristic of the Cartesian mode. Because we are slaves not only to our limited powers of perception but also to our mental habits, our scientific inquiry is in constant danger of becoming not only neurotic in its repression of what we arbitrarily regard as irrelevant to our inquiry at hand but also psychotic in its distortion of what we perceive in reality space in formulating our models of reality.

Themes and Variations

The Freudian conception of human action as resulting from psychic reality suggests that no mode of theorizing about reality can be completely independent of the cultural and other *a priori* that those who seek knowledge acquire in their psychic life. Thus science is not always an impartial human endeavor to obtain knowledge. This Freudian suggestion about the potential bias in the scientific approach to reality was actually a healthy development in the history of ideas. As a matter of fact, the post-Freudian sciences do exhibit a bit of Freudian relativism in their formulations of the nature of reality.

We may begin our brief review of the post-Freudian contributions to knowledge with Einstein. What is remarkable about the Einsteinian mode of theorizing about reality is the idea that relativity is indeed the essential feature not only of psychic reality but also of physical reality. While time was granted a special status as an absolute frame of reference for all physical events in classical physics, Einstein demonstrated, with his special theory of relativity, that time has no absolute significance: "Every reference-body (coordinate system) has its own particular time; unless we are told the reference-body to which the statement of time refers, there is no meaning in a statement of the time of an event" (Einstein

[1916], p. 26). Thus beginning with Einstein, time appears merely as one of the coordinates of a four-dimensional space-time continuum, a sort of malleable frame of reference in which physical events take place. The special theory also replaced the Newtonian postulate about the existence of an absolute, privileged position to study the laws of nature with the Einsteinian postulate about the relativity of the observer with respect to the natural phenomena to be investigated. The fundamental role measuring instruments play in the special theory further suggests an alternative way of interpreting the Einsteinian mode of theorizing about reality. If we think of measuring instruments as extensions and refinements of our perceptive faculties, the Einsteinian mode points to an important way in which action space, which is linked to perception space through the act of measuring, is embedded in reality space, i.e., $Z = g(Y) \subset X$. Moreover, the general theory of relativity, with its cosmic constant, introduced the possibility that reality space as our physical universe has a history, capable of continually expanding or contracting—a surprising yet natural extension of the Darwinian conception of reality space.

> With the advent of quantum mechanics, our belief in the certainty of our scientific theories has come to be seriously challenged. With the Cartesian objectification of reality space, scientists used to be certain about the objective validity of their theories of reality once these were confirmed by empirical verification. Heisenberg challenged this Cartesian presupposition by first questioning the validity of the independence of different causes acting simultaneously (Heisenberg [1958]). In particular, his "uncertainty principle", in its original form, introduced a theoretical limit on the accuracy with which certain connected quantities at the atomic level, like the position and momentum of a particle, can be simultaneously measured.

Heisenberg's uncertainty principle has subsequently been generalized as an expression of uncertainty about the complete neutrality of the scientist from the phenomena to be investigated. In other words, the generalized Heisenberg principle states that our act of knowing, which belongs to action space, is, in an essential way, embedded in reality space, i.e., $h(X_i) \cap X_i \neq \phi$. Although the lack of certainty implied by the Heisenberg principle is regarded as a feature of small-scale events, its philosophical implications are far-reaching in that it suggests a possible interaction between mind and matter, a possibility which was completely neglected by the Cartesians. The presence of such interaction should not come totally as surprise; the further we go into a smaller unit of analysis, whether it be the decomposition of mind or the quantum mechanics of matter, the further we enter the realm where events in reality space are influenced by the elements of chance.

Wiener's contribution to knowledge, in one sense, can be regarded as an extension of the Cartesian mode of theorizing about reality, for cybernetics can be interpreted as an empirical verification of the Cartesian metaphor of man as a machine (Wiener [1948]). In another, it can be regarded as an extension of the Darwinian mode of theorizing about reality with a Freudian twist. It is one thing to say that man is like a machine but quite another to develop a machine which would actually replace a human faculty, especially if that faculty turns out to be "human intellect". For one thing, the development of machines which can replace human intellect has brought about a new kind of social change whose impact is expected to be extensive and complex. Aside from its social impact, the reason why Wiener's contribution can be regarded as an extension of the Darwinian mode of theorizing about reality with a Freudian twist is that we are talking here about machines which replace human intellect rather than human muscle. Note, however, that these machines can also be interpreted as extensions of our perceptive faculties—indeed our linkage to the unconscious. Whatever gap there is between reality space and action space, perception space aided by artificial intelligence promises to stretch our ordinary powers of perception and to unveil to us a kind of reality which has hitherto been accessible only to those with extraordinary powers of perception. Granted that artificial intelligence can stretch human intelligence, one question still remains: Is it possible to expand action space, with its linkage to perception space aided by artificial intelligence, to such a degree that it actually covers the entire reality space? To put it formally, is it ever possible to have $Z=g(Y)=X$?

Two contributions made in this century in mathematics may shed some light on this question. One contribution comes from the area of pure mathematics in the form of Gödel's incompleteness theorem (Gödel [1962]). What Gödel shows is that there is a "logical gap" in our logico-deductive mode of theorizing about reality. As such, the incompleteness theorem exposes the vulnerability of the Cartesian mode which relies solely on the deductive method of reasoning. Here we are confronted with a paradoxical situation in which the very act of theorizing has unveiled the inherent limitation of theorizing. If there are aspects of reality, as suggested by Gödel's incompleteness theorem, which cannot be ascertained by logical reasoning, what will? If complete knowledge of reality is what we strive for and if theorizing will not get us there, what recourse is left for us but to revert to perceiving?

Rene Thom's theory of catastrophe offers an interesting illustration of the usefulness of the Freudian mode of free association and may lead to a resolution of the Gödelian dilemma inherent in our theorizing (Thom [1975]). The Freudian mode of free association is exploited to full advantage in the theory of catastrophe not only in its formulations, which connect several branches of mathematics, but also in its applications in different branches of science. In particular, the principle of catastrophic equivalence has uncovered many connections among different phenomena which have hitherto been unnoticed as totally unrelated. The patterns of connections which appear in the principle of catastrophic equivalence are not, however, in terms of quantitative relationships but rather in terms of qualitative properties such as forms and shapes. In the principle of catastrophic equivalence we thus witness a clear break away from the Cartesian rationalist tradition in the history of ideas, the tradition within which Gödel operates.

It is interesting to note that, with Thom's catastrophe theory, we have gone full circle in our discussion of "the mode of theorizing and the nature of knowledge". It was Descartes, it is recalled, who introduced the idea that forms and shapes, which are geometric properties of things, can be transformed into algebraic equations with the use of the coordinate system which he invented. What Descartes accomplished with his algebraic and analytic representations of reality, Thom accomplishes with his geometric and topological representations. The principle of catastrophic equivalence thus signals the return of the power of perceiving the geometric and topological properties of things as a key to our knowledge of the world around us.

The Organic Mode

It is now time to take stock and develop a mode of theorizing about reality which would unify the different modes, themes and variations discussed in the preceding pages. The unified mode we propose may be termed the "organic mode"—organic in the sense that the process of knowledge acquisition is in conformity with the process of human development. It is important to relate knowledge acquisition to human development because, when it comes to knowledge acquisition, there is no getting around Protagoras' dictum: "Man is the measure of all things." The dictum is particularly pertinent here because what we are concerned with is not so much what the world around us is like as how we go about acquiring knowledge of the world around us.

The Cartesian mode of theorizing about reality, in addition to the drawbacks discussed already, is also seriously flawed because it takes no account of the development of our perceptive faculties, including our bodily faculties, which aid in our subjective experience of the world around us. After all, reason is an important mental faculty which we cultivate during the process of human development. Moreover, human development does not take place in a vacuum; it is a process of constant interaction between the individual and the environment. Following the pioneering work by Erikson in this field, the space of human development can be discussed in terms of the biological, social and psychological processes (Erikson [1950]). By the biological process of human development we mean the development of physical functions and physiological faculties in the individual, including the development of the central nervous system housed in the brain. By the social process we mean the development of social consciousness and technical skill which the individual needs if he is to function as a societal member, and by the psychological process the development of psychological and other cognitive faculties which the individual needs in order to make sense of reality around him.

The idea of representing human development as taking place within the space of ecological interaction among the biological, social and psychological processes for man as an individual can be extended to represent human evolution as taking place, in a similar fashion, within the space of ecological interaction among the biological, social and psychological processes for man as a species. In fact, the body of our scientific knowledge of the world around us, which we have accumulated over the centuries ever since Descartes ushered in the age of democracy in knowledge acquisition, can be exploited to define the space of human evolution which we need for our unified mode of theorizing about reality.

To be specific, the space of human evolution can be defined as the space of ecological interaction among the biological, social and psychological processes, except that these processes are now defined in the context of the phylogeny of man. First, the biological process of human evolution can be conceived as taking place within the space of ecological interaction between "life" and "matter", for man as a biological being comes into contact with both organic elements (life) and inorganic elements (matter) in the environment.

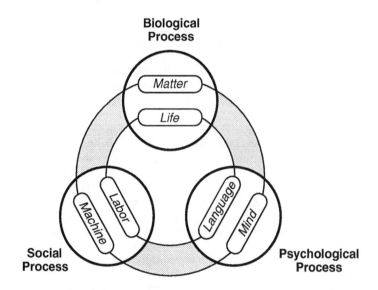

Next, the social process of human evolution can be conceived as taking place within the space of ecological interaction between "labor" and "machine", for man as a social being must confront the crucial economic question of how to organize labor and machine in the production and distribution of goods and services. The Marxian mode of theorizing about social reality as revolving around the infrastructure of labor and machine as a symbolic representation of opposing social forces, though somewhat contrived, still provides a useful insight into the sometimes violent nature of the social aspect of human evolution.

Finally, the psychological process of human evolution can be conceived as taking place within the space of ecological interaction between "language" and "mind", for man as a psychological being depends on the use of language and other symbols for his mental development. The Freudian mode of theorizing about psychic reality is pertinent here because language holds a key not only to unraveling of our psychic past but also to communication of our knowledge of the world to other societal members.

Our unified mode of theorizing about reality can now be defined in terms of the space of human development at the ontogenetic level and that of human evolution at the phylogenetic level. In the first place, the space of human development defined as the space of ecological interaction among the biological, social and psychological processes for man as an individual is identified as action space, which is linked to perception space through the mapping called "acting". Then, the space of human evolution defined as the space of ecological interaction among the biological, social and psychological processes for man as a species is identified as reality space. With these specific interpretations of reality, perception and action spaces, our unified mode of theorizing can be couched within the analytical framework of human action which we have used throughout our discussion in the preceding pages.

There are at least three conditions which our unified mode must satisfy if it is to qualify as the "organic mode". The first condition is already incorporated in our definition of reality, perception, and action spaces. In particular, it should be clear from the way these spaces are related to the spaces of human development and evolution that the subjective act of learning and knowledge acquisition takes place in the space of human development which is embedded in the space of human evolution. In other words, our definitions incorporate an important condition, $Z = g(Y) \subset X$, which has become an essential feature of the mode of theorizing we have inherited since Darwin's original insight into the nature of human existence as a species. This condition may be termed the condition of "organic consistency". It states that human existence both as an individual and as a species must be consistent in the context of evolution as reality space. Or, to put it slightly differently, it states that whatever we perceive or do as human beings is made consistent by evolution which provides the context in which all things in reality space, including ourselves, are united.

The second condition which the organic mode must satisfy may be termed the condition of "organic coherence". In order for human development to be organically viable, there must exist some kind of interdependence among the three constituent processes. Interdependence is important because all three aspects of human development—physical as well as mental, inherited as well as acquired, intuitive as well as logical—aid in the subjective act of learning about the world around us. Formally speaking, the condition of organic coherence may be stated as: $N(z^1(t), z^2(t), z^3(t)) = 0$, where $z^1(t)$ is a vector of variables representing the biological process at time t, $z^2(t)$ a vector of variables representing the social process at time t, and $z^3(t)$ a vector of variables representing the psychological process at time t. Our formalism simply means that human development as a temporal process must take place on a manifold in the space of ecological interaction among the biological, social and psychological processes. In other words, there must exist a certain degree of complementarity among the three processes if human development is to be organically viable. The condition of organic coherence for human evolution can be similarly defined as: $M(x^1(t), x^2(t), x^3(t)) = 0$, where $x^1(t)$, $x^2(t)$ and $x^3(t)$ are given similar interpretations as above except that these vectors are now defined in the context of human evolution as a species. The condition of organic coherence is our way of stating that nature has no leaps.

The third condition for the organic mode may be termed the condition of "organic correspondence". Organic coherence implies that there exists a correspondence in the sense of an interdependence among the three constituent processes both for human development and evolution. Because action space is embedded in reality space, we would expect the existence of other correspondences between ontogeny and phylogeny, between the process of human development and that of human evolution. In analogy with biological evolution, some may be tempted to appeal to the theory of recapitulation to argue for the existence of such correspondences. However, correspondences come about not because of recapitulation but because both human development and evolution are organic processes defined in the context of evolution. Formally, organic correspondences may be stated as: $X_i \sim Z_i$, where X_i and Z_i are appropriate subspaces of X and Z, and '$\sim$' denotes "correspondence".

Correspondence here is to be interpreted mainly in terms of topological invariance and catastrophic equivalence. For example, the aging process, which applies to both the individual and society, is known to be characterized in terms of the fold catastrophe. And the cycle of manic-depressive episodes for individuals and that of war-peace episodes for nations can be explained in terms of the cusp catastrophe.

The important question here is, of course, why such correspondences exist. Rene Thom postulates the existence of what he calls *champ vital*, which may be interpreted as a unified field of all events in reality space. Systems theorists may explain such correspondences in terms of structural similarities among various systems. Thus, James Miller talks about a hierarchy of living systems in his *Living Systems* (Miller [1978]). Bateson, on the other hand, appeals to the correspondence between the mind and the universe as far as their organization as systems is concerned (Bateson [1979]).

In the context of our inquiry, such correspondences exist because both human development and human evolution are organic processes unified in the context of evolution as reality space. In fact, it is because of evolution that we have the continuity of life in which individual lives come and go as different manifestations of the same underlying reality. Or, to borrow a more poetic metaphor from T.S. Eliot, "we are the music while the music lasts."

Conclusion

The Cartesian mode of theorizing about reality has influenced the evolution of modern societies ever since Descartes ushered in the age of democracy in knowledge acquisition. In particular, the Cartesian mode, with its segmentation of reality space, its dichotomization of perception space and its separation of action space, has transformed the world into a disorganized entity—with knowledge being pursued by specialists who guard their areas of specialty with a zeal approaching territorial instincts, with human development being constantly disrupted by segmented systems of education, and with our natural environment being willfully manipulated to advance myopic interests of one social group or another.

The organic mode of theorizing about reality is designed to remove these defects of the Cartesian mode while at the same time retaining its strength in studying specific aspects of reality. It is a mode of theorizing which views the world as an organic process whose consistency, coherence and correspondence among different parts and layers are defined in the context of evolution. Most importantly, it is a mode of theorizing which treats knowledge acquisition as a process in conformity with the process of human development taking place in the space of human evolution.

That the organic mode requires consistency, coherence and correspondence has definite implications for educational and other social institutions which aid human development. The condition of organic consistency states that the space of human development as action space must be embedded in the space of human evolution as reality space. In other words, what we have been, what we are, and what we can be as human beings, are all made meaningful only in the context of human evolution. This condition thus sets the ultimate bounds for our perceptions and actions. Cultivating our potential within the bounds imposed on us by the forces beyond our control is what human development is all about and assisting this process should be the sole aim of educational and other social institutions. The condition also implies that we are ultimately responsible for what we do as human beings. As all our actions are contained in reality space, whatever we do as human beings to our environment, natural as well as human, will have consequences coming back to ourselves. Scientists are no exception to this, for this condition is our way of incorporating the generalized Heisenberg principle.

The condition of organic coherence is especially important in rethinking the role of social institutions in human development. The human child, during the process of its ontogenetic development, comes into contact with many social institutions whose aim is to assist this process—families, nurseries, schools, churches, government agencies, courts, and, alas, prisons. The role of these social institutions under the organic mode must be one of maintaining the organic coherence of the individual by preventing him from becoming disoriented in the world around him. The intrusion of professionals with the Cartesian mentality into the process of human development can be actually harmful as it leads to the loss of organic coherence of the individual concerned. Too many bits of advice given by too many experts can only add to his confusion and will lead to a loss of identity on his part, which is a symptom of a lack of organic coherence.

The condition of organic coherence as applied to the space of human evolution similarly points to the need for maintaining an ecological balance among the biological, social and psychological processes of human evolution. The loss of organic coherence in the space of human evolution is perhaps the most serious damage inflicted on the world by excessive applications of the Cartesian mode of theorizing. Mismanagement of our natural environment, manipulation of other people's lives, and vicious cycles of conflict among ethnic groups and nation-states are but a few examples of the lack of organic coherence that we witness in the world today. What the condition of organic coherence calls for is simply an awareness that our very existence as a species depends on delicate balancing of the biological, social and psychological processes around us and within ourselves. Indeed, not only do we live in the world but we are also being allowed to live by the world.

The condition of organic correspondence, which states the existence of correspondences among different parts and layers in the space of human evolution, constitutes the negation of the atomistic view of the world. Thus society is not simply a nominal entity defined as the sum of individuals. Society is a "real" entity in the sense that individuals are guided by social consciousness which resides in their psychic reality. While social realism has been misused in the past as a source of social control, the kind of realism implied by the organic mode, to the extent that it is backed by our awareness of reality as an organic whole, is a precondition for social order, let alone social harmony. The condition of organic correspondence, carried to its natural conclusion, implies the existence of a correspondence between man as an individual and man as a species. Ultimately, whether such correspondence is translated into a species consciousness to guide individual actions holds the key to our continued existence as a species.

2. ZEN, RELATIVITY AND THE AESTHETICS OF NO-ACTION

Introduction

Creating tension between action and no-action, between motion and rest, plays a vital role in all forms of Japanese art. How such tension is created, needless to say, differs from one form of art to another. In the performing and martial arts, which involve bodily movement, the artist deliberately resorts to no-action in the literal sense of the word. In fact, mastering the art of controlling one's body and mind at the critical moment of no-action when all motion is frozen is generally regarded as a mark of highest artistic achievement.

There is no reason, however, why the aesthetics of no-action should be limited to the performing and martial arts; a state of no-action would not command the aesthetic value that it does in Japanese art if it were employed in only those forms of art which involve bodily movement. Although the meaning of the word "no-action" needs to be interpreted in a figurative sense, the same artistic ideal is pursued in other forms of art as well. A master artist is one who, regardless of the artistic medium employed, is able to convert a state of no-action into one of high drama, full of imagery and suggestion.

An outstanding example of the effective use of no-action in visual art is Hokusai's woodblock print, "The Great Wave". As is true with any work of art which is recognized as a masterpiece, this work is never short of those qualities which appeal to our sensibility. Some may be awed by the sheer immensity of the wave, which is about to break and engulf precariously floating boats. Others may feel sympathy towards the people who are helplessly clinging to the swaying boats. Still others may be struck by the lively composition of the scenery highlighted by the use of bold lines.

"The Great Wave", to be sure, evokes all these feelings and sensations. But what is most remarkable about it is the skill with which Hokusai managed to create tension between action and no-action, between motion and rest, which is vital to Japanese art. For what Hokusai so masterfully captured is a movement temporarily frozen, a drama which is temporarily halted. As a result, we, the viewers, are thrust right into the uncharted space which lies between hope and despair, between life and death. Indeed, this work reminds us of the unsettling condition of our existence, of our frail endeavors against natural forces. All this existential anxiety crosses our minds in a flash as we view this world of wind, waves and clouds—we are mere bubbles in the cosmic sea of mutability! How much, indeed, this work tells us about ourselves!

Hokusai's masterpiece thus exemplifies what the aesthetics of no-action is all about. For one thing, the aesthetics of no-action expresses an artistic ideal which cherishes economy of effort on the part of the artist in bringing out the maximal effect. More importantly, however, it reflects a state of high artistic achievement in which the artist, by recreating reality, becomes one with reality. But what does the aesthetics of no-action mean to us moderns who have long lost touch with such an intuitive mode of comprehending reality? This is the question we hope to explore in this chapter.

Zen and the Aesthetics of No-Action

No form of Japanese art incorporates the aesthetics of no-action more explicitly than the Noh play. This is so not only because the Noh performance deliberately blends action and no-action, but also because Noh as an art form is founded on a definite set of aesthetic principles. We can infer what these principles are, thanks to Zeami, the principal figure in the development of Noh, who left us a number of critical essays on this art form.

The main aesthetic principle underlying Noh, according to Zeami, is *yugen*, which roughly translates into "mystery" or "profundity". To be more specific, *yugen* is the term that characterizes the state of highest achievement in the Noh play as embodied in the beauty of form and movement. In Zeami's own words, *yugen* refers to "a degree of artistry which is of that middle ground where being and non-being meet" (Zeami [1958], p. 295).

The influence of Zen Buddhism is apparent in these words. Noh, as a performing art, tries to recreate human drama which invariably involves tension between the pain of life and the stillness of death; this tension defines the middle ground between being and nonbeing, between life and death. How, then, does the Noh performance propose to guide the audience into this middle ground? This is where the aesthetics of no-action comes into play, as we find in the following words of Zeami: "Dancing and singing, movements and the different types of miming are all acts performed by the body. Moments of 'no-action' occur inbetween. When we examine why such moments without actions are enjoyable, we find that it is due to the underlying spiritual strength of the actor which unremittingly holds the attention. He does not relax the tension when the dancing or singing comes to an end or at intervals between the dialogue and the different types of miming, but maintains an unwavering inner strength. This feeling of inner strength will faintly reveal itself and bring enjoyment. However, it is undesirable for the actor to permit this inner strength to become obvious to the audience. If it is obvious, it becomes an act, and is no longer 'no-action'. The actions before and after an interval of 'no-action' must be linked by entering the state of mindlessness in which one conceals even from oneself one's intent. This, then, is the faculty of moving audiences, by linking all the artistic powers with one mind" (Zeami [1958], p. 291).

We can infer from these words that the moments of no-action acquire their importance, in the first place, from the importance of integrating the body and the mind. While the body engages in all kinds of actions in the performing arts, the mind unifies these actions by interspersing them with moments of no-action when the body is at rest. This is the way in which the tension between action and no-action, between motion and rest, is created in the Noh play. As a matter of fact, Zeami goes a step further by suggesting that the moments of no-action are the most enjoyable part of Noh. Here we find further evidence of Zen influence in which the mind is interpreted as the unifying principle of the cosmic process. To see how Zen philosophy underlies Noh, we must examine in more detail some of the characteristic features of Noh as a performing art.

There are many features of Noh which we can easily identify as Zen elements. First, there is the idea of simplicity which regulates the staging of the Noh play. Although the costumes worn by the Noh actors are often colorful and elaborate, reminiscent of the artistic ideal of *miyabi* which characterized Heian court life, the Noh stage itself is a simple, rectangular structure. Moreover, the stage is usually left completely bare except for small gadgets called *tsukurimono* which are employed in some plays. This is one way of conveying to the audience that Noh relies heavily on the power of suggestion. The simplicity of the setting is reinforced by the simplicity of actions and movements. Unlike the ballet dancer, the Noh actor, as a rule, is not expected to stand on tip-toe or leap in the air. In fact, the whole performance is expected to be one of graceful restraint, as if to evoke the stillness beyond this world. The Noh actors often wear the masks of ghosts, suggesting that the audience is being invited to glimpse into another reality. The drama itself usually revolves around the theme of existential anxiety which is created by the tension between the pain of life and the stillness of death.

There is another interesting feature of Noh which reminds us of the Zen emphasis on the mind as the fundamental unifying principle. In Noh plays, the Buddhist monk plays the major role in pacifying the spirits of the ghosts who, having failed to find salvation themselves, return to this world to haunt the people with whom they used to associate in their former lives. The priest, with his enlightened mind, guides the ghosts to attain salvation as the drama draws to a close. From a psychological point of view, Noh actually offers an interesting resolution of the conflict between *animus* and *anima* in the human mind by introducing three archetypal roles—the warrior, the woman, and the old man. In this triad, the old man, often appearing as a Buddhist priest, embodies the archetype of the wise old man in Jungian psychology. It is, therefore, possible to give a psychological interpretation to the aesthetics of no-action in Noh in terms of Jungian psychology as invoking "Self", the all-embracing aspect of the working of the unconscious mind (Jung [1969]).

If the mind is indeed the unifying principle in Noh plays, then the audience is expected to appreciate the world of *yugen* staged by these accomplished actors by participating in the drama with their own minds. As Zeami states, "what the mind sees is the essence; what the eyes see is the performance" (Zeami, [1958], p. 302). In that the ghost plays a major role, *Hamlet* comes closest to creating the world depicted in Noh, especially in those Noh plays which are called ***mugennoh***. Recall how Hamlet's mind was able to see his father in that middle ground where being and nonbeing meet. If the aesthetics of no-action carries an epistemological implication, it thus comes down to this simple statement: What the mind sees is the essence; what the eyes see is the performance. Then, did not the fox remind the Little Prince, "It is only with the heart that one can see rightly; what is essential is invisible to the eye" (Exupery [1971], p.87)? In the state of mindlessness which characterizes the moments of no-action, Noh actors can guide the audience into that middle ground between being and nonbeing. For it is the mind that links all things—being and nonbeing, life and death, past and present.

What is true in Noh is also true in other forms of art. The aesthetics of no-action as an aid to knowledge explains why the ink-brush painting called *sumie* makes copious usage of empty space. The empty space, unlike the negative space in Western painting, carries positive meaning, as the space of no-action. It is here in the empty space that the painter appeals to the power of suggestion to draw our attention to the things which are not depicted in the painting. Moreover, a master painter like Sesshu skillfully employs a flexible perspective to guide us right into the middle ground between being and nonbeing. Take a look at any one of Sesshu's landscape paintings. The whole scenery evokes such an eerie sensation that we are made to feel as if we are floating in the air, travelling over mountains and waters. This must be the kind of sensation which Wordsworth experienced when he wrote:

> I wandered lonely as a cloud
> That floats on high o'er vales and hills

(Wordsworth [1936], p.149). By letting our minds escape into the scenery painted by a master painter, we are guided into the middle ground between being and nonbeing and rewarded with "the bliss of solitude" which flashed upon Wordsworth's inward eye.

In literature, the aesthetics of no-action involves inferring the hidden meaning between the lines. What is left out between the lines in the space of no-action often becomes more important than what is actually written. This explains why the Japanese have elevated *haiku*, a poem consisting of only 17 syllables, into one of the highest forms of art. To appreciate what is expressed in a *haiku*, we are expected to project ourselves into the world the author creates within and beyond the span of 17 syllables. The more we are able to infer what is left unsaid, the more we are able to experience the totality of reality which covers both the space of action and of no-action. Here again we are reminded of the all-important epistemological implication of the aesthetics of no-action: It is the mind that links all things—being and nonbeing, life and death, past and present.

Relativity and the Aesthetics of No-Action

The aesthetics of no-action as an artistic ideal lends itself to a natural interpretation as expressing the importance of economy of effort on the part of the artist. In the performing and martial arts which involve bodily movement, this interpretation has an obvious linkage to the physics of the body in motion. Does the aesthetics of no-action as an aid to knowledge, which has to do with the working of the mind, have a similar linkage to the physics of the body in motion? To make any sense out of this question, it may be useful to rephrase the question as follows: What does it mean to say that something is in a state of no-action, or rest?

A little reflection should convince us that there is no such thing as something being absolutely in a state of no-action. Consider, for example, the case of the Noh actor who is in a state of no-action when all his dancing and singing come to rest. To the audience this state of no-action of the Noh actor is perceived as a state of no-action relative to the stage on which his performance is taking place. But what if the Noh play in question is being staged on a boat moving on a lake? To the audience who is on the moving boat watching the performance, a state of no-action of the Noh actor continues to be perceived as a state of no-action. However, to a person standing on the shore, the same state of no-action would no longer appear as a state of no-action, for the stage, or the boat on which the Noh performance is taking place, is moving relative to the shore on which this person is standing. Is the person standing on the shore, then, in a state of no-action? By now it should be clear that the answer has to be: "It depends." If we define his act of standing with respect to the shore, or the earth, he is in a state of no-action. However, neither he nor the earth would be in a state of no-action relative to the sun around which the earth revolves. Even the sun, if we follow this line of reasoning, will not be in a state of no-action relative to some galaxy.

This is exactly the kind of reasoning, it may be recalled, that led Einstein to formulate his theory of relativity. It is not difficult to see why this kind of reasoning leads to a notion that the only motion in the physical universe is motion relative to something else. Einstein developed this notion into his special theory of relativity because he found it difficult to accept, in the face of the Michelson-Morley experiment which confirmed the constancy of the speed of light, the old Gallileian notion about the existence of a body of reference which is physically at rest. If he was to rescue the principle of relativity, which guarantees that the same laws of nature apply in all bodies of reference moving uniformly relative to each other, he had to abandon the Gallileian transformation in favor of the Lorenz transformation. All this, of course, is well known to the student of the history of science. What concerns us here is the question, What does the Einsteinian special theory of relativity, which has to do with the physics of the the body in motion, have to say on the aesthetics of no-action, which has to do with the working of the mind in the state of mindlessness?

The nature of the relationship between the special theory of relativity and the aesthetics of no-action may become clearer if we go back and examine the meaning of two basic postulates of the special theory: the principle of relativity and the law of propagation of light. The principle of relativity says that the laws of nature are the same in all bodies of reference moving uniformly with respect to each other. Because the only motion in the physical universe is motion relative to some body of reference, the principle of relativity implies that there is no way of distinguishing between uniform motion and non-motion. The law of propagation of light, on the other hand, says that the velocity of transmission of light in a vacuum is the same in all bodies of reference for all observers moving uniformly relative to each other. The law implies that the instruments used to measure distance or time change from one body of reference to another in such a way that the speed of light always appears to be constant at 300,000 km/second. How a given moving object will appear to an observer will therefore depend on whether the observer is stationary or moving with the object. To a stationary observer, a moving object measures shorter, distance-wise as well as time-wise, as its velocity increases.

These implications of two basic postulates of the special theory of relativity have corresponding implications for the aesthetics of no-action. That a state of no-action is, as was already argued in the case of the Noh actor, only relative to some body of reference follows from the principle of relativity. To the performing artist, therefore, a state of no-action means that the artist is at rest relative to the stage on which the performance takes place. However, because the stage itself is also moving relative to some body of reference, it follows that the artist in a state of no-action can actually experience being in a state of motion. To those in the audience who are watching the performance, the same state of no-action provides an opportunity to duplicate the artist's experience by projecting themselves into the same space of mindlessness, as they are encouraged to do in the Noh performance.

That appearances are relative, on the other hand, follows from the law of propagation of light. If appearances are relative, then it is up to the mind to discern the reality behind changing appearances. In fact, in the case of the performing and martial arts which involve bodily movement, the artist's mind and body must be in harmony if he is to experience, firsthand, that to be in a state of no-action is to become a part of the cosmic process. Dogen, the founder of the Soto school of Zen in Japan, also talks about the importance of integrating our body and mind if we are to discern the reality behind the veil of relativity: "When you go out on a boat and look around, you feel as if the shore were moving. But if you fix your eyes on the rim of the boat, you become aware that the boat is moving. It is exactly the same when you try to know the objective world while still in a state of confusion in regard to your own body and mind" (Dogen [1958], p. 252).

The special theory of relativity, which has successfully integrated two basic postulates, has further interesting implications. First, there is the equivalence of mass and energy expressed by the celebrated formula: $E=mc^2$. The formula says that mass and energy are different manifestations of the same thing, that mass is nothing but a form of stored energy. Because energy is released with action, the equivalence of mass and energy has an interesting implication for the aesthetics of no-action. In particular, it implies that a state of no-action corresponds to a state in which there is no energy due to velocity. This, then, provides us a physical basis for the statement that the aesthetics of no-action involves economy of effort on the part of the artist. Another interesting implication of the special theory of relativity follows from the Einsteinian body of reference, or coordinate system, which involves the concept of a four-dimensional space-time continuum. This concept provides us with a physical basis for the importance of here and now. Carried to its extremity, the concept implies that here contains there and everywhere, and now contains past as well as future. A state of no-action here and now, in the light of the concept of a four-dimensional space-time continuum, thus carries a far-reaching epistemological implication as holding a key to knowledge. T.S. Eliot (Eliot [1971], p. 16), with his characteristic flair for rhythm, beautifully expresses what this knowledge is all about:

> Time past and time future
> Allow but a little consciousness.
> To be conscious is not to be in time
> But only in time can the moment in the rose-garden,
> The moment in the arbour where the rain beat,
> The moment in the draughty church at smokefall
> Be remembered; involved with past and future.
> Only through time time is conquered.

Zen Buddhists, too, emphasize the importance of here and now, for Zen is not so much an abstract system of thought as an idea that every act of living holds a key to knowledge. As a practical method of acquiring knowledge, however, Zen Buddhists have come to stress the importance of meditation, for meditation in the act of sitting, for example, helps us to guide ourselves into the state of mindlessness. The Zen emphasis on meditation also reflects their conception of the mind as the unifying principle of the cosmic process. But this does not mean that the body can be neglected. On the contrary, the body plays an equally, or probably more, important role in reaching enlightenment as Dogen explains: "So long as one hopes to grasp the Truth only through the mind, one will not attain it even in a thousand existences or in eons of time. Only when one lets go of the mind and ceases to seek an intellectual apprehension of the Truth is liberation attainable. Enlightenment of the mind through the sense of sight and comprehension of the Truth through the sense of hearing are truly bodily attainments. To do away with mental deliberation and cognition, and simply to go on sitting, is the method by which the Way is made an intimate part of our lives. Thus attainment of the Way becomes truly attainment through the body" (Dogen [1958], p. 255).

The aesthetics of no-action thus lends itself to an interesting physical inter-pretation whether we look at it as a phenomenon associated with the physics of the body at rest or the psychology of the mind in the state of mindlessness. Historically speaking, the aesthetics of no-action in Japanese art has evolved out of Zen philosophy and, therefore, expresses the Oriental ideal about the impor-tance of being in tune with the cosmic process which is also found in Taoism. The Taoist concept of *wu wei*, which is usually translated as "non-action", does not mean, therefore, doing nothing. Rather, it means action in harmony with the ongoing cosmic process. This is what Lao Tsu means when he says, "Tao abides in non-action, yet nothing is left undone" (Lao Tsu [1972], p.39). In the final analysis, the aesthetics of no-action is thus an outgrowth of a worldview which emphasizes the need for human existence to be in harmony with the cosmic process.

Conclusion

The aesthetics of no-action as an artistic ideal cherishes economy of effort on the part of the artist in bringing out the maximal effect. To the extent that art imi-tates life, the aesthetics of no-action thus incorporates a notion of "economy" which is to be cherished in conducting our lives. To be more specific, the notion implies that our lives must be in tune with the cosmic process, that a true econ-omy lies in maintaining an organic harmony with nature.

The aesthetics of no-action as an aid to knowledge, on the other hand, sug-gests a holistic approach to comprehending reality. It is holistic, first, in the sense that both the mind and the body are involved in the acquisition of knowledge of the world around us. This is in sharp contrast to the Cartesian paradigm, which employs a reductionistic methodology based on an arbitrary segmentation of reality. The aesthetics of no-action explicitly recognizes the ecological nature of reality which includes ourselves as part of the cosmic process. While the Cartesian paradigm tries to understand nature by separating nature from ourselves as an object of our rational inquiry, the aesthetics of no-action tries to comprehend nature by placing us right in the midst of the cosmic process. While the Cartesian paradigm guides us to study the laws of nature which govern the cosmic drama, the aesthetics of no-action guides us to learn the ways of nature by participating in that drama.

Our comment here is not to be construed as a rejection of a reductionistic approach to knowledge as represented by the Cartesian paradigm. Because reality involves complicated patterns of ecological interaction, an artificial segmentation of reality becomes a useful device of acquiring knowledge about different aspects of reality. By doing so, however, we tend to lose sight of reality as an organic whole of which we are a part. If we moderns have come to lose a sense of unity with nature, it is partly because we have relied too much on science as an aid to knowledge which treats nature as an object of rational inquiry separate from ourselves. By separating nature from ourselves, we have lost the sense of belonging to nature, which comes from the realization that we, too, are the product of the cosmic process.

The aesthetics of no-action, in contrast, is a way of acquiring knowledge while preserving that sense of belonging to nature. By using art to recreate reality, we are trying to create the mirror of perception in our own minds, which would reflect ourselves as part of that reality. The aesthetics of no-action is thus intended as an aid to developing the mind necessary to reach enlightenment by overcoming the constraints which the body imposes on us by confining ourselves to here and now.

Finally, the aesthetics of no-action, as it relies on artistic symbolism, is patently a non-linguistic mode of representing reality. Any attempt to represent reality by a linguistic mode is, in the final analysis, limited by the cardinality of the language which is employed to describe reality. Science is no exception in this regard. The aesthetics of no-action, on the other hand, explicitly recognizes the importance of comprehending reality *in toto*, which is beyond the cardinality of any language. According to Lao Tsu, "The Tao that can be told is not the eternal Tao" (Lao Tsu [1972], p. 39). Our own endeavor to describe what the aesthetics of no-action is all about now finds itself in a state of no-action where words no longer suffice. With Hamlet, we conclude, "The rest is silence."

3. MIND, CONSCIOUSNESS AND KNOWLEDGE:
East and West

Introduction

Our fascination with the workings of our own minds has a long history. Beginning with such old masters as Socrates and Plato in the West and Buddha and Lao Tzu in the East, generations of great thinkers have reflected on the question of how the minds of us mere mortals are capable of grasping the mysteries of the world around us. In fact, the question of mind, consciousness and knowledge seems to have acquired renewed interest among philosophers and scientists in recent years with advances in Artificial Intelligence and cognitive sciences.

While scientific research has greatly expanded our understanding of the way our minds work, we have yet to integrate the latest findings of science with insights obtained by our old masters in philosophy and religion and develop a unified view of mind, consciousness and knowledge. Developing a unified view is important because both the rational tradition of the West and the intuitive tradition of the East agree that integrating our knowledge of self and of the world leads us to enlightenment and liberation. The purpose of this chapter is to examine what kind of unified view emerges when findings of Western science and insights of Eastern thought are integrated. Teachings of old masters in the Eastern tradition will be examined in the light of recent advances in Artificial Intelligence and cognitive sciences.

The Western Tradition

The concept of "mind" in the tradition of Western philosophy and science arises in relation to such concepts as "reason", "thought", "intellect", "consciousness", "understanding", and "purpose". All these concepts suggest that mind, as it relates to knowledge acquisition, is seen in the Western tradition as an agent of purposeful and highly intellectual activity. Such a rational conception of mind is indeed one salient feature of the Western tradition which has been carried on by philosophers and scientists to this day.

Another feature of the Western tradition is an uneasy tension that exists between the mentalist and the physicalist conception of mind—the tension which dates back to Descartes' dualistic conception of mind and body. While the mentalists consider "mind" as an agent of pure thought which can lead its separate existence from the body, the physicalists treat it as an extension of man's physical organs. Starting with the British empiricists, such as John Locke who considered sensory experience as the only reliable source of knowledge, the physicalist tradition is still alive and well and is pursued vigorously by neuro-physiologists and behavioral psychologists. To the physicalists, consciousness is simply an epiphenomenon of the workings of the material brain. The mentalist tradition, too, has its contemporary adherents in such figures as J.A. Fodor [1975] and Sperry [1983]. Sperry, for example, considers consciousness as an active and operational force capable of triggering events in the material brain.

Needless to say, many philosophers and scientists have attempted to resolve the tension between the mentalist and the physicalist conceptions of mind. For example, Kant proposed his resolution by distinguishing between the physical world, or the world of things in themselves, and the phenomenological world, or the world of appearances. The human mind was then seen as an active agent that mediates between the two worlds, an agent that guides us to knowledge of the world around us. Another resolution is suggested by evolutionists, among whom we may count such diverse figures as Aquinas, Darwin, Piaget, and Jaynes. To them the human mind is like *tabula rasa* in its original state but acquires perceptive and cognitive capacities as the individual develops biologically, psychologically and socially (Piaget [1970], Jaynes [1980]).

Starting with Turing's challenge which ushered in the age of computers and artificial intelligence, cognitive scientists and philosophers have developed a new, "functionalist" view of mind. This view suggests still another resolution of the tension between the mentalist and the physicalist conception of mind. According to the functionalists, the physical characteristics of the machinery are less important than its "functional organization" (Putnam [1975]). To the extent that thinking and other intelligent functions can be carried out, human minds, machines and animals can all be regarded as being capable of "mental" activities. And to the extent that human minds and computers work in a similar manner, i.e., to the extent that minds and machines are functionally equivalent, there is no reason why we have to attach special significance to knowledge that accrues to the human mind. To borrow Minsky's expression, the human mind is but one member of the society of mind (Minsky [1985]).

The rational tradition of the West, which associates mind with reason and intellect, has long regarded consciousness as an almost exclusive agent of knowledge acquisition. However, the past century has seen some notable changes in this Western outlook on mind and consciousness. First, there was the Freudian revolution. Since Freud, Western philosophers and scientists have come to accept the influence of the subconscious mind on human behavior. In fact, Freud was ready to accept "animism", though primitive, as a system of thought, a *Weltanschauung*, which gives a complete explanation of the world (Freud [1913]). With the advancement of researches into Artificial Intelligence, Western philosophers and scientists are now seriously entertaining the possibility that consciousness may comprise only a small part of mind and that knowledge can indeed come from the unconscious workings of mind, human or non-human (Gardner [1985]). Recognizing the contribution of the totality of mind to knowledge acquisition actually brings the Western tradition very close to the Eastern tradition.

The Eastern Tradition

The concept of mind in the Eastern tradition arises in relation to such concepts as "awareness", "senses", "contemplation", "taming", "cleansing", and "emancipation". Mind is thus conceived holistically as encompassing both mental awareness and physical senses. And the Eastern approach to knowledge is intuitive, in contrast to the rational tradition of Western philosophy and science. One reason for this is that philosophy and science in the East, until their contact with their Western counterparts, had not been clearly separated from religion, with all three contributing to the total effort to seek knowledge.

WEST	EAST
REASON	INTUITION
INTELLECT	INSIGHT
IMAGINATION	CONTEMPLATION
SOUL	BODY
SPIRIT	EMANCIPATION
CONSCIOUSNESS	MINDFULNESS
PSYCHE	SENSES
MEMORY	CLEANSING
UNDERSTANDING	ENLIGHTENMENT

The dualism between mind and body, the tension between the mentalist and the physicalist conception of mind, is indeed foreign to the Eastern tradition. Even when there is dualism, like that between *yang* and *yin* in Chinese thought, the relationship between two elements is not one of tension but of complementarity. The same can be said of the relationship between mind and body. Integrating different aspects of human faculties, both mental and physical, is regarded as holding the key to knowledge in Eastern philosophy and religious thought.

This is evident in the work of Asanga who founded the Yogacara school of Buddhism. The goal of Buddhism as religion is to achieve liberation from attachment to life in this world, which is full of pain and suffering. And generations of Buddhist philosophers have developed diverse systems of practical guides for behavior, including Buddha's own Noble Eightfold Path, which can be employed for ordinary people to achieve liberation by acquiring total knowledge of the world. In the case of Asanga, a system of physical exercises is recommended in order to fully cultivate all the senses available to us. To be specific,

Asanga talks of six senses of seeing, hearing, smelling, tasting, touching, and thinking. To these are added *mana-vijnana*, or ego consciousness, and *alaya-vijnana*, or cosmic consciousness, which is the storehouse of consciousness containing all the traces of past actions as well as the potentialities of future actions. The cultivation of all human senses through a series of bodily exercises enables us to join *mana-vijnana* with *alaya-vijnana*, thus leading us to knowledge and to liberation.

Another figure worth noting in the Eastern Buddhist tradition is Kukai, a Buddhist monk who founded the Shingon sect of esoteric Buddhism in Japan. Kukai developed his theory in his work, *Shoji-Jisso-Gi*, compiled in the early part of the ninth century. To Kukai mind is the totality of the space of interaction between what he calls "six dusts" and "six senses". Six dusts are: color, voice, smell, taste, touch, and *dharma*. They represent visual, auditory, olfactory, sensory, tactile and "meaningful" stimuli in the environment. Six senses are: eye, ear, nose, tongue, body, and consciousness.

SIX DUSTS	SIX SENSES
COLOR	SEEING
VOICE	HEARING
SMELL	SMELLING
TASTE	TASTING
TOUCH	TOUCHING
DHARMA	CONSCIOUSNESS

Note that *dharma* is regarded as one of the stimuli, suggesting that there are mental as well as physical stimuli in the world around us. Consciousness is regarded as one of six senses, the part of our senses which has to do with our mental faculties while others refer to the senses associated with our physiological faculties. Needless to say, these mental and physical faculties need to work in tandem if knowledge of the world is to be obtained. Thus, by cultivating the workings of all the senses, which involves rigorous physical exercises, we are able to reach an awakened state, fully mindful of all the stimuli in the environment, and thus achieve liberation by acquiring knowledge of the world around us. In systems parlance, knowledge of the world around us requires synergistic cooperation of all of our mental and physical faculties.

Common to these and other Eastern thinkers is the idea that both the mental and physical faculties are involved in the acquisition of knowledge. They thus call for the cultivation of all our mental and physical faculties. In this holistic conception of mind and body, the Eastern tradition rejects the metaphysical illusion of modern Western science that knowledge can be obtained by the power of logical reasoning alone. This is true even of Confucius who is regarded as the founder of the rationalist tradition in Eastern philosophy. The anti-rational position is carried to the extreme by Zen Buddhists who reject the rational conception of mind as illustrated by their use of *koan*, or puzzle, as an aid to knowledge.

Mind, Consciousness and Knowledge: East and West

The relationship among mind, consciousness and knowledge is fairly straightforward if, as has been the case in the Western tradition, knowledge acquisition is seen mainly as an activity of the conscious mind. Knowledge, in such a conception, results from a highly specialized activity of "mind"—and a highly localized activity of the brain at that.

The Eastern tradition, in contrast, treats consciousness as but a small part of "mind". As such, consciousness plays only a limited role in knowledge acquisition. Knowledge thus results from the total activities of "mind", conscious as well as unconscious. Among modern Western scientists Jung is the sole exception in his holistic approach to knowledge when he talks about the interplay of four faculties of thinking, feeling, sensation and intuition (Jung [1969]). In fact, the Jungian conception of "individuation" as the goal for human development is quite similar to the goal of enlightenment in Mahayana Buddhism which requires integration of *Atman* and *Brahma*, of ego and Self.

There is also an interesting parallel between William James and Asanga when James talks about the world of present consciousness as being only one out of many worlds of consciousness that exist (James [1958]). Asanga would only add that there is a way to make linkages among James' many worlds: by joining *mana-vijnana* with *alaya-vijnana*. Sperry's hypothesis about consciousness being a real causal agent in the brain process also has a parallel in Kukai's idea that *dharma* serves as one stimulus which triggers responses in mental as well as physiological senses. Indeed, when we exclude *dharma* and consciousness and focus our attention on the relationship between five kinds of stimuli and five kinds of senses, Kukai can well pass as a behaviorist.

Western scientists have long resisted the idea that the unconscious mind plays a key role in knowledge acquisition. Jung is, again, an exception to this. But lately we find more and more Western scientists accepting the positive role of the unconscious mind. For example, Polanyi talks about the role of the "tacit dimension" (Polanyi [1966]). And modern researchers in Artificial Intelligence such as Minsky, with his acknowledgement of the workings of the unconscious mind in humans as well as in machines, come very close to embracing Eastern philosophy.

The very essence of the Eastern tradition is the idea that mind *is* the unifying principle of the cosmic process of which we are a part. As Buddha says: "All states have mind as their fore-runner; to them mind is supreme and of mind are they made" *(Dhammapada)*. To the Buddhists, then, the cosmic process is a mental process which entails unfolding of minds. It is comforting to find some Western scientists, notably Gregory Bateson, who are ready to accept the idea that evolution is a mental process (Bateson [1979]).

Conclusion

Convergence between the rational tradition of the West and the intuitive tradition of the East is indeed taking place as the mysteries of mind are increasingly unveiled to us by research in cognitive sciences. The challenge we face now is whether such convergence will lead to the emergence of a new view of the world, a new *Weltanschauung*, which is eminently humane in its conception of the human mind and harmonious in its treatment of man's relation to the natural environment.

When findings of Western science and insights of Eastern thought are integrated, what emerges is the conception of mind as a process which is defined in the space of interaction among our mental and physical faculties. As such, mind obviously has both the subjective part and the universal part, for mind, in this conception, is a product of evolution and thus partakes in the cosmic process called "nature".

A view of mind which emerges out of a synthesis of the Western and the Eastern tradition does point to an integrated theory of mind, consciousness and knowledge. This does not mean that the totality of the knowledge of the world around us is now readily available to us. Both Western and Eastern masters warn us that "strait is the gate, and narrow is the way" to knowledge. We may not yet know how to get there, but at least we can start to speculate what it is like to be there.

PART TWO

INDIVIDUAL AUTONOMY AND

SOCIAL ORDER

4. HUMAN AUTONOMY AND SOCIAL COHESION

Introduction

Every society needs some type of steering and control if it is to function as a viable system. To the extent that steering and control are involved, society can be regarded as a cybernetic system. The fact that society is a cybernetic system is at the root of all the controversies about human autonomy. Needless to say, autonomy in the sense of the individual having complete control over his affairs is an illusion which must be dismissed if humans are to live in a society. So the real question is, as it has always been, "In what sense, and to what extent, is man autonomous?"

To derive a meaningful answer to this question, we need to examine the condition of human existence in its biological, psychological, and social dimensions. This is so because man is a system whose existence is defined in the space of interaction with his natural, psychological, and social environment. The nature of interaction between man and his environment determines the sense in which man is autonomous and the extent to which he is able to exercise that autonomy.

Man as a system is surrounded by other systems—individuals, groups, associations, communities, nations, international organizations, and the global system called "nature" (Homans [1951]). Man is an open system with respect to these other systems. The pattern of his interaction with these other systems will differ from one system to another. We must therefore be prepared to accept the diversity in the meaning of autonomy.

The Meaning of Autonomy

In what sense is man an autonomous being? Since man is a system whose "being" is defined in the space of interaction with his natural, psychological, and social environment, we may begin by examining the sense in which man is a biological being, a psychological being, and a social being.

The sense in which man is a biological being can be summarized by the following postulate:

Postulate I (**Man as a Biological Being**): Man is a biological being in the sense that his existence depends on the exchange of matter and energy with the natural environment.

The postulate simply restates a biological fact that man is a living system whose survival depends on the intake of food and other substance from the environment. Since this is a restatement of a biological truism, the constancy of "internal milieu" developed by Claude Bernard may be adopted as a relevant concept of autonomy (Vendryes [1987]).

Man, like other living organisms, employs a feedback control process over the reserves of matter and energy in order to maintain the constancy of "internal milieu". Autonomy for man as a biological being thus corresponds to the concept of "homeostasis" in physiology (Cannon [1939]).

What distinguishes man from other living organisms is the fact that his behavior is guided by psychological faculties over and beyond his animal instincts. This point can be summarized as follows:

Postulate II (Man as a Psychological Being): Man is a psychological being in the sense that his actions are reflections of psychic realities.

Human actions reflect all kinds of drives, motives and incentives. The totality of these "psychic realities" which trigger human actions can be thought of as defining man's psychological states. Man is thus an open system with respect to his psychological environment as some of these psychological states are defined in his interaction with other human beings. The space of psychological states can be regarded as having both depth and extension. That is, some actions are the results of the psychological states to be located near the surface of the psychological states while others are reflections of the psychological states buried in a wider and deeper realm, i.e., the unconscious as opposed to the conscious realm of psychic realities.

It is fruitful to conceive, as we are doing here, each of man's actions as reflecting a specific psychological state. That part of his actions for which he has an awareness of intentions, motivations and, to some extent, consequences can be regarded as defining his "ego boundary" (Brix [1986]). The concept of the "ego boundary" is the psychological counterpart to Bernard's concept of the "internal milieu" and defines the boundary which man, in his psychological life, employs to maintain autonomy freed from the influence of other human beings.

Autonomy in the psychological sense of the term can thus be defined in terms of the constancy of the ego boundary. Man is an autonomous being, psychologically speaking, as long as he is guided by the conscious ego in his actions, being aware of motives and intentions behind, and consequences of, these actions.

The fact that we are using "ego" as a guide for behavior means that psychological autonomy is a feature that we expect from a "mature" human being. Ego, which enables us to draw the psychological boundary from other individuals, is something that comes with maturation, for the child, in the early phases of development, fails to distinguish between the inside and the outside world (Piaget [1954]). That psychological autonomy is related to human development has an important social implication, for human development takes place in a social setting.

All human actions are performed by individuals as societal members, except for an individual who chooses to lead a solitary existence *a la* Robinson Crusoe. Man is a social animal and this aspect of human existence can be summarized by the following postulate:

> *Postulate III* (**Man as a Social Being**): Man is a social being in the sense that his existence involves interactions with other individuals in his cultural, economic and political life.

The above postulate contains a definition of society as a system. That is, society is seen as a system consisting of "culture", "economy" and "polity". Since society is a system which consists of these subsystems, defining autonomy for man as a social being becomes a complicated proposition.

Man leads cultural life in the sense that he participates in the creation and dissemination of values, symbols and ideas. Man shares some values with one group of individuals but violently rejects certain other values held by another group of individuals. In cultural life persuasion and coercion are often employed to convert others to accept certain views. Defining autonomy in cultural life thus requires suitable modification of the concept of the "ego boundary" in the choice of cultural values, symbols and ideas.

Autonomy for man as an economic being can be defined by adapting the concept of the constancy of the internal milieu introduced above in the context of our discussion of man as a biological being. Man leads economic life in that he participates in the production and distribution of goods and services. Except, again, for the case of a Robinson Crusoe, man cannot lead his economic life without engaging in a variety of transactions with other human beings in order to maintain—and expand—his reserves of capital, widely interpreted to include physical, financial as well as human capital. However, since not everybody has the same access to capital, society can severely limit, for some people, their ability to maintain reserves which are needed for economic autonomy. Because of the inequitable nature of the distribution of reserves, human relations in the economic arena can be subject to manipulation and control. The realities of economic life aside, economic autonomy can be defined, conceptually, in terms of the constancy of the reserves of capital which constitute the internal milieu for man's material existence.

Autonomy of man in his political life, by definition, requires a participatory democracy. For, once the individual's right to participate in decision-making in social affairs is relegated to a representative government, his political life becomes subject to bureaucratic control of one sort or another. This raises an interesting question of whether a participatory democracy is at all possible except on a small scale for a local community. Development in communications technologies does help the situation greatly by expanding the scope of participation. Then, we must be concerned with the question of who controls those communications technologies, meaning that political autonomy is inherently tied up with economic autonomy.

Coordinating Autonomy in Different Spheres of Human Existence

The fact that man is at the same time a biological being, a psychological being and a social being means that there is no uniform concept of autonomy which applies to all three aspects of human existence. This is so because, although man is an open system relative to his environment, the manner in which he interacts with his environment is qualitatively different from one type of environment to another. Thus, it becomes necessary for us to distinguish among biological autonomy, psychological autonomy, and social autonomy.

The lack of uniformity does not mean that a unified science of man is not possible. Biological, psychological and social aspects are not separate and independent spheres of human existence. There is interdependence among the three spheres of human existence and the existence of interdependence implies that autonomy in one area has a certain correspondence with autonomy in another. For example, metabolic autonomy and mental autonomy are related to, if not completely controlled by, the functioning of the brain.

The most important linkage among the biological, psychological and social aspects of human existence is provided by the fact that they are different aspects of the same process called human development. Thus, it is possible, theoretically at least, to coordinate among different aspects of autonomy in relation to human development. Needless to say, there is no guarantee that human development for any individual is a coordinated process, for the biological, psychological and social aspects of human development are, by themselves, neither complementary nor synchronized. Biological and psychological developments are complementary to some extent in that human development involves development of both the body and the mind. There is no guarantee, however, that the social aspect of human development will be in harmony with the other two aspects of human development.

One reason why natural (i.e., biological and psychological) and social developments may conflict with each other is that society develops laws and institutions at the aggregate level which often impede individual human development (Bronfenbrenner [1979]). One illustration of this is the lack of uniformity in our laws concerning the age at which the individual reaches maturity. Thus, different minimum age requirements are imposed on drinking, driving, voting and seeking employment. Variations across individuals in the process of maturation complicate the problem still further.

If social constraints impede human development and thus limit the exercise of human autonomy, why do we need them? The answer is that autonomy for an individual can be potentially harmful to the common interests of all individuals. In other words, allowing maximal autonomy at the individual level may well lead to the loss of autonomy at the aggregate level—of a group, of an organization, of a nation or, for that matter, of humankind as a species. This is the problem known as "the tragedy of the commons" (Hardin [1968]). If we are to avoid falling into the pitfall of the tragedy of the commons, we must develop the concept of autonomy which is relevant to the workings of the whole system, i.e., "system autonomy".

Conclusion

Traditional discussions of human autonomy are deficient in that they are either expressed as a political ideal or described as one type of equilibrium of a micro entity. Autonomy in the sense of a political ideal would be very difficult to maintain in a social system in which man is an open system relative to other individuals and organizations, which is the case even in a liberal democratic society. On the other hand, autonomy in the sense of the constancy of one sort or another for a micro entity is untenable if autonomy at the micro level leads to the breakdown of autonomy at the aggregate level.

What all this means is that human autonomy can be meaningfully discussed only in the context of a systems view of man (Bertalanffy [1981]). Man is a system whose existence is defined in the space of interaction with his biological, psychological and social environment. Given this reality of human existence, one essential ingredient of "system autonomy" would be "organic coherence" among the biological, psychological and social aspects of human development. To this autonomy at the micro level of individuals must be added the concept of "organic correspondence" which ensures that autonomy at the micro level would not lead to the breakdown of autonomy at the aggregate level of societies (Koizumi [1990]).

The fact that the social aspect of human development is something that is artificially imposed on individual human development means that coordinating between social and individual human development is of the utmost importance in assuring "system autonomy". What kind of social system will ensure "system autonomy" in the sense of satisfying both "organic coherence" and "organic correspondence" is a difficult question for which there may well be no answer. If that were the case, autonomy at the individual level could only be defined in stochastic terms. Indeed, if no social system could guarantee "system autonomy", then the only resolution of the paradox of human existence would be the one Nietzsche suggested: "Man must be overcome!" Being aware of this is, of course, one road to liberation, if not to autonomy.

5. CULTURE AND SOCIAL ORDER

Introduction

Matthew Arnold defined "culture" as "the pursuit of perfection" in his *Culture and Anarchy* published in 1869 (Arnold [1924]). This definition, obviously very different from the standard definition of culture given by anthropologists, is distinctly a modern product of European intellectual history. In fact, in this conception of culture as the pursuit of perfection Arnold was joined by such notable figures as Carlyle and Ruskin in England and Goethe and Nietzsche on the Continent.

The idea that these humanists were promoting was the idea of culture which would reflect the inner urge of the human mind to seek refinement and wisdom. As Arnold put it, it was the idea of culture as "the pursuit of sweetness and light". With such a conception of culture, Arnold and these humanists were attempting to restore the "culture" of harmonious life in nineteenth-century Europe as opposed to the "anarchy" of disorganized life. Their attempt was also a reaction to what they perceived to be the European preoccupation with regimentation and control in economic life which was spreading into other areas of social life. This preoccupation was driving the general populace into misery and disarray instead of bringing them prosperity and social harmony.

Arnold and these humanists were thus deeply concerned about the general, mechanistic outlook on life that was gaining ground on the European scene in the nineteenth century. And their concern actually went beyond mere sentimental reminiscence of the old way of life that had prevailed before the Industrial Revolution or, for that matter, romantic retreat into the serenity of the country life. They—and Arnold in particular—were interested in the possibility of appealing to culture as a means of restoring social order which, they felt, was being undermined by the overzealous pursuit of industrialism, despite the promise it held for political democracy and economic progress.

Society as a System of Social Actions

What is the relationship between culture and social order? If we are to derive any sensible answer to this question that can be used as a guide in formulating cultural policy, we must first ask what is meant by society, for social order is, presumably, a certain feature of a functioning society. Moreover, since we are particularly interested in the relationship between culture and economy as one aspect of social order, it is useful to think of society as a system which contains culture and economy as subsystems. To be more specific, we follow the work of Parsons and Shils and define society as an abstract space of human actions, some of which take place in the realm of culture and others in that of economy (Parsons and Shils [1952]). Formally, we can express this idea as follows:

> *Postulate I* (**Society as a System of Social Actions**): A society is a system consisting of social actions which include cultural and economic actions as integral components. That is, $S = \{X, Y, T\}$, where $X = $ '*culture*', or the set of all human actions pertaining to the creation and dissemination of ideas, symbols and values, $Y = $ '*economy*', or the set of all human actions pertaining to the production and distribution of goods and services, and $T = $ '*time*', or the set of all integers.

Postulate I incorporates a simple idea that society exists in the space of all social actions. "Culture" and "economy" are introduced as the basic subsystems of society. "Time" is introduced here as the frame of reference for all actions. This device will become useful later when we discuss the dynamic evolution of a social system. In particular, society will be seen as a system which evolves over time in the space of interaction between "culture" and "economy".

We do not introduce "polity" as a separate subsystem of a social system because policy-makers are also seen as participants in "culture" and "economy" as the formulators of cultural and economic policies. How the policy-makers can or cannot influence social actions will be discussed in more detail later.

Our conception of society as a system as expressed in Postulate I does not see society as consisting of various social groups and organizations. These can be brought in when we explore the social implications of cultural and economic actions as occupying "significant" subsets of the sets of cultural and economic actions. In fact, according to Postulate I, each cultural or economic action is a social action in that both culture and economy are embedded in society and, therefore, acquires its social meaning in the context of a specific social institution such as the family, the school, or the workplace.

Postulate I, defined as it is in abstract terms, contains such unwieldy terms as the set of all cultural actions and the set of all economic actions. In order to make our analysis operational both theoretically and empirically, it is important that these sets be represented by concrete, empirically meaningful variables. This requirement of "representability" can be expressed formally as follows:

> *Postulate II* (**Representability**): A social system at any given time can be represented by a finite number of social variables. That is, given a social system $S = \{X, Y, T\}$, there exists a mapping
>
> $$[x(t), y(t)]: 2^X \times 2^Y \rightarrow R^m \times R^n \text{ for every } t \text{ in } T.$$

The postulate of representability states that a finite number (m for culture and n for economy) of social variables $[x(t), y(t)]$ can be chosen from the social action space $\{X, Y\}$ at all times to represent the state of the underlying social system.

These variables may be regarded as "phenotypes" in the evolution of a social system, or "revealed characteristics" of the set of all social actions. Although finite numbers are chosen, we are not suggesting that a single, all-purpose social variable ("the" social indicator, if you will) can be constructed to represent the state of the underlying social system. Some degree of aggregation may be necessary, however, in constructing certain variables. For example, to the extent that the gross national product (GNP) is considered the most comprehensive measure of the performance of the aggregate entity called the national economy, it may be chosen as one of the social variables.

We now incorporate into our analysis some important systemic features of society which need to be reflected as the revealed characteristics of a "real" social system. Given Postulate II, the evolution of a social system can be represented by the social process vector $\{x(t), y(t); t \varepsilon T\}$. First, we incorporate an important property of an evolutionary system that such a system invariably undergoes qualitative changes over time. In the context of our discussion, this feature can be formally expressed as follows:

Postulate III (Transmutation): The social process is subject to transmutations from past actions. That is, for every t in T there exists

(i) a $p_i(>1)$ and a g_i such that

$x_i(t) = g_i[x(t-1), Y(t-p_i)]$ for at least one i in $\{1, 2, ..., m\}$,

where $Y(t-p_i) = [y(t-1), y(t-2), ..., y(t-p_i)]$, and

(ii) a $q_j(>1)$ and a h_j such that

$y_j(t) = h_j[y(t-1), X(t-q_j)]$ for at least one j in $\{1, 2, ..., n\}$,

where $X(t-q_j) = [x(t-1), x(t-2), ..., x(t-q_j)]$.

The postulate of transmutation, (i), incorporates the idea that economy influences culture in the sense that the kind of ideas and values the members of a society develop and adhere to may be affected by past economic actions. A transmutation of the cultural process may occur within a subsystem (i.e., a specific cultural institution such as a family, a theater, or a museum) or may cover the whole system of cultural actions. A transmutation of the cultural process often takes the form of a particular economic practice influencing the *modus operandi* of cultural institutions. For example, in a society where competition in the economic arena rewards the aggressive and the ruthless, administrators of such cultural institutions as art museums, opera companies and even charitable organizations cannot afford to be meek and pure in heart if they are to compete effectively with business organizations in the same economic arena.

Similarly, the postulate of transmutation, (ii), incorporates the idea that culture influences economy in the sense that the current economic practices often reflect the ideas and values formed in the past. As with the transmutation of the cultural process, the transmutation of the economic process may occur within a specific economic organization such as a firm or a banking house, or may encompass the whole economic process. The role of the Protestant ethic in economic development discussed by Tawney and Max Weber is a classic example of the transmutation of the economic process (Tawney [1926], Weber [1930]).

The postulate of transmutation explicitly recognizes the presence of dynamic interaction between culture and economy and the sometimes unpredictable nature of that interaction. If events in the evolution of a social system are sometimes unpredictable, every society strives to maintain its viability amidst various disturbances which constantly threaten to drive it into disintegration—even extinction. Put differently, the fact that a social system is viable at any given time is evidence that there are those individuals in society who are concerned about the viability of their society and translate their concern into various social actions. This point can be expressed formally as follows:

> *Postulate IV* (**Viability as Organic Coherence**): The viability of a social system implies the existence of organic coherence among component variables in the social process. That is, if a social system $S = \{X, Y, T\}$ is viable at t in T, then there exists a f such that $f[x(t), y(t)] = 0$.

The postulate of viability as organic coherence incorporates the idea that a certain degree of complementarity exists among component variables of the social process if a social system is viable. The phenomenon of economic development points to the importance of organic coherence, for economic development is a social process which requires coordination and cooperation of many cultural and economic activities. The lack of organic coherence in the form of an excessive and unbalanced growth of one particular variable often foreshadows a catastrophic change in a social system. One illustration of this is the German hyperinflation of the 1920s which led to the rise of a totalitarian regime in that country. Put still differently, the postulate of viability as organic coherence says that a society which is functioning maintains some kind of balance among the diversity of its actions.

Finally, we need to say something about the role of the public sector in a social system. If the social process is not reducible to a single, all-purpose social indicator, the job of public administrators in managing a social system is made that much more difficult. Since Postulate II precludes such reducibility except possibly when $X=Y$, public administrators need to observe more than one social variable in order to assess the effectiveness of their policy. The problem is further complicated by Postulate III which negates the possibility that any policy will remain purely cultural or economic for any extended period of time. All this implies that the public sector, or the government, can at best be an active participant of the social process. Thus, we have:

> *Postulate V* (**Polity as Subsystem**): Polity is embedded in a social system and cannot exist as a transcendental entity. That is, there is no subsystem in S with its action space R such that $X \cup Y \subset R$.

The postulates I through V together define the framework of analyzing the evolution of a social system in general and the nature of interaction between culture and economy in particular. It is also the framework which we propose to employ in investigating the nature of the relationship between culture and social order.

Culture and Social Order

Arnold and other humanists were led to formulate their humanistic conception of culture as a reaction to the wave of industrialism which was swallowing up European societies in the nineteenth century. Such reaction can be interpreted as an expression of their concern over what they perceived to be the lack of organic coherence in their societies. To Arnold and other humanists, European societies in the nineteenth century were too preoccupied with the pursuit of material progress prompted by a mechanistic outlook on life which they had inherited from previous centuries. The prevalence of a mechanistic outlook on life can be regarded as an instance of what we defined above as a transmutation of the economic process. And a transmutation of the cultural process was also taking place as the preoccupation with regimentation and control in the economic arena was now spreading into the cultural arena.

Arnold's conception of culture as the pursuit of "sweetness and light" is testimony to his concern over the erosion of those ideas and values which he regarded as essential for the harmonious development of the human self. These ideas and values were being transmuted by the ideas and values which had gained influence in the economic arena, depriving the individual of an awareness of the totality of his existence and thereby undermining the foundation of a civilized society. The latter half of the nineteenth century thus saw the culmination of a social process which had started in eighteenth-century England—separation of culture from economy. As long as culture meant, as Arnold saw it, the totality of human actions pertaining to the pursuit of sweetness and light, it had no longer much in common with economy, or the totality of human actions pertaining to the production and distribution of goods and services.

Arnold's view of English society as consisting of three classes of Barbarians, Philistines and Populace illustrates the degree to which culture was separated from economy in nineteenth-century England. While culture was pursued by Barbarians, or the aristocracy, with their lofty ideals and distinguished manners, the conduct of economic affairs was left to Philistines, or the middle class, with their preoccupation with the accumulation of material wealth. Finally, Populace, because of their low station in society, was completely left out of the mainstream of the social process. In short, English society, as Arnold saw it, was characterized by division and headed towards anarchy.

Separation of culture and economy is one sign that a social system lacks organic coherence. Since both culture and economy refer to spheres of human action, the lack of organic coherence at the societal level can be traced back to the realm of human psychology. If culture refers to the realm of human actions with their aim directed towards the pursuit of sweetness and light, it is separated from economy where human actions are motivated by the pursuit of greed and self-interest. And as long as culture and economy are driven by these different psychological motives, it becomes difficult for a social system to maintain its organic coherence.

The concept of organic coherence provides one context in which the question of social order can be meaningfully discussed. The presence or absence of organic coherence will be reflected on the f function in Postulate IV, which may be termed the "form" of a social system. To be more precise, the "form" of a society is defined by the set $F = \{[x(t), y(t)]: f[x(t), y(t)] = 0\}$.

Postulate IV also contains a statement about the role of the government in the evolution of a social system. This is so because the actions of policy-makers and the effects of their actions are already incorporated in the "revealed form" of a social system in Postulate V which views the government as, at best, an active participant of the social process. Put differently, although society is a system, it is not strictly a cybernetic system in the sense that it can be subjected to conscious steering and control of the government. Society is a system only in the sense that the totality of human actions in society leads to some type of coherence at the aggregate level if it is functioning.

Our discussion of the form of a social system above does not include any statement about the type of f function which defines, in one sense or another, a desirable feature of a social system. The question of a desirable society, needless to say, belongs to the realm of value judgment which we are not prepared to discuss at this point. Moreover, even if such a desirable form of a social system were identified by the government, it would lack resources to guide society into this form in view of the implications of our postulates. The system of five postulates thus reflects our conception of what a liberal democratic society is all about where the government is prohibited from imposing a specific value system on the general public. This does not mean, however, that the government cannot influence the course of the evolution of a social system. How the government might influence the direction of the social process will be discussed next in reference to the conduct of cultural policy.

The Dilemma of Cultural Policy

If cultural policy is one component of the government's social policy, we would expect it to be geared towards the promotion of the common good of society. Granted that there are difficulties in defining what constitutes the common good, it is a bit disturbing that the conduct of cultural policy in the U.S.A. and Europe, as reported in many empirical studies, seems to be directed towards the promotion of special interests (Waits, Hendon and Horowitz [1985]). One reason cited for this is that the cultural sector does not produce the type of goods which economists classify as purely public. If cultural goods are not purely public, then they are subject to the exclusion principle, thus depriving some members of society from the benefits of those cultural goods which happen to be provided. On the other hand, to the extent that cultural goods are public, the general public may not exhibit their demand for them, thus making it difficult for policy-makers to determine what type of cultural goods ought to be provided.

As long as cultural goods are not purely public, any argument employed to justify the production of specific cultural goods, or the support of specific cultural activities, ends up promoting special interests. This is certainly the case with the benefit-cost analysis applied to a specific cultural activity. For one thing, it is difficult to conduct the benefit-cost analysis in a truly general equilibrium context, evaluating the full impact of a specific cultural activity on society. For another, the benefit-cost analysis suffers from the lack of uniform and universal criterion by which benefits and costs are added up. As such, it is likely to be manipulated to justify a specific cultural activity.

The "earnings gap" argument, developed by Baumol and Bowen, does try to incorporate a general equilibrium perspective in that it proposes to support those cultural activities which cannot generate enough earnings to match the earnings of other productive sectors of the economy (Baumol and Bowen [1966]). This argument, however, seems to take it for granted that a cultural activity, like any other activity, must be subjected to the same economic criterion of productivity and profitability if it is to justify its existence in society. Moreover, if the decline in the earnings of some activities is a result of taste changes on the part of the general public, it is difficult to justify public support for these activities as long as society is committed to the principle of market capitalism as an organizing principle of the economy.

As things stand now, economic analyses are applied to promote special interests as they are employed by those cultural groups and organizations whose goals and missions in society are to protect and promote specific cultural activities. In a way economics is caught in a quandary which Adam Smith foresaw when he defined political economy as "a branch of the science of a statesman or legislator" (Smith [1937]). Since sovereignty in a democratic society lies with the people, economics is employed as the science of every citizen, every group, and every organization. And when economics is employed as a means of justifying a specific cultural activity, it is employed to promote a specific value system despite its neutral stance towards values as a scientific discipline.

The way economic analyses are employed today in the formulation of cultural policy is a reflection of the fundamental dilemma of liberal democracy. As symbolized by the posture of separation of church and state, the government in a liberal democratic society, in principle, refrains from imposing a specific value system on the general public. This means that any group or organization interested in promoting a specific value system must do so in the context of the political process. In practice, this means that such a group or an organization engages in political lobbying of one sort or another in order to secure political support for its activity.

The profusion of lobbying activities combined with the ineffective and sometimes inconsistent application of public policy makes a liberal democratic society especially susceptible to transmutations of the social process, thus undermining the organic coherence of a social system. Whether cultural policy leads to the protection of the public interest and promotes the common good of society depends, in the final analysis, on whether the general public, including policy-makers, who participate in the making of the social process do so with sufficient concern over the organic coherence of their society as a system.

Conclusion

Social philosophers do not speak with one voice when it comes to the question of the proper relationship between culture and social order. On the one hand, we have a philosopher like Plato who considered maintaining social order to be more important than guaranteeing the freedom of artistic activities. Thus he argued for a ban on all poetry except hymns to gods and praises of famous men, which presumably contribute to the maintenance of social order. On the other hand, we have a philosopher like J.S. Mill who strongly advocated the freedom of the arts from both secular and ecclesiastic authorities. For him the arts and the sciences were part and parcel of one's liberty to create, to express, to argue and to know. Thus the freedom of cultural activities was something which ought to be protected by the government.

The humanistic conception of culture, as it views culture as the pursuit of perfection with one's conscience as the sole guide, tends to view any type of cultural policy with suspicion. Paradoxical as it may sound, such an attitude is actually what is needed for a democratic society to function as a system while maintaining its organic coherence. For, in order to prevent the government from imposing a specific value system, it is essential that each and every citizen possess the inquisitive mind of a scientist and the detached eye of an artist.

Whether culture can contribute to social order must eventually be discussed in the context of human development. To the extent that no single individual or entity oversees the direction of the evolution of a social system in a liberal democratic society, it becomes essential that each individual develop an awareness that individual human actions in culture and economy are embedded in a larger context of a social system and that the viability of that social system depends crucially on whether the totality of individual human actions will lead to some kind of coherence at the aggregate level. If nothing else, the humanistic conception of culture provides one framework for cultivating such awareness.

6. KNOWLEDGE, POWER AND DEMOCRACY

Introduction

Democracy, despite its popular appeal as a principle of organizing social life, has not always received unconditional endorsement from social philosophers as an ideal form of government. Ever since Plato characterized it as "the worst of all lawful governments and the best of all lawless ones", generations of social philosophers have expressed their concern over the feasibility of a democratic form of government. Their concern centers around the fact that democracy demands a great deal from the people who are the sovereigns in this form of government. As James Madison put it, democracy demands that "the people...arm themselves with the power which knowledge gives" (Rossiter [1961], p. 34).

The lack of proper understanding of the sense in which knowledge is the source of power for the people is indeed the reason why democracy fails to live up to its expectations, leading a precarious existence as it oscillates between tyranny and anarchy. Even in societies of the West where democracy is regarded as working successfully, a democratic form of government has not been immune from serious criticism and reexamination in recent years. Some have gone as far as characterizing the situation as the crisis of democracy, citing such symptoms as the misrepresentation of the people's will in foreign policy, the decision overload, the immobility of the bureaucratic machinery, and the loss of trust and confidence in political leadership (Crozier et. al. [1975]).

Whether one agrees with the use of the term "crisis" to characterize the state of affairs democratic societies find themselves in today, democracy has indeed come to exhibit symptoms of dysfunction in many areas of social life. It is important, then, to examine how and why democracy has come to suffer various symptoms of dysfunction despite what many regard as "knowledge explosion" which has taken place in the evolution of modern democratic societies. What we are confronted with is a paradoxical situation in that the accumulation of knowledge which has taken place in the last few centuries, instead of arming the people with power, has come to undermine the effectiveness of democratic societies in organizing social life.

The Dysfunction of Modern Democracy

The dysfunction of democracy is most conspicuous in societies which adopt a representative form of government. This is to be expected because the power, which the people are supposed to exercise over the course of social affairs, is diluted in a representative democracy. Social decisions are made by the representative body which, despite its announced commitment to implementing the will of the people, tends to represent and therefore promote the narrow special interests of one social group or another.

Many authors and commentators have pointed out that too much power is concentrated in the executive branch of the government, especially in the area of foreign policy where the democratic process of translating national interests into a coherent national policy is often bypassed in the name of swift and timely action in the international political arena. Foreign policy aside, many authors have pointed out that it has become virtually impossible today to arrive at a national consensus on a social issue, however important that issue may be (Dahl [1982], Toffler [1980]). Liberal democratic societies in particular have seen the disaggregation of group interests and the diffusion of cultural values in recent years. The upshot is that majority rule, which is considered almost sacred as a method of resolving social conflict in democratic societies, no longer serves as a workable mechanism as majority support is seldom obtained for any social issue (Staub [1980]).

The difficulty of obtaining majority support, let alone a consensus, is compounded by the ever-increasing number of problems over which the government is asked to make decisions. There are a number of reasons why this decision overload problem has come to inflict representative democracies. One reason is found in the area of economy where the government has been called upon to play an expanding role in the management of the national economy. Since the Great Depression of the 1930s, many industrialized countries have adopted the maintenance of a high and stable level of employment as an integral aspect of the government's social policy. The government has also been increasingly involved, partly as a way of resolving social conflicts, in promoting economic growth and in redistributing the fruits of economic growth in an equitable manner among the population.

Once the government takes upon itself the role of a patron who caters to the needs—economic or otherwise—of the people as clients, many groups of individuals such as unions and professional associations begin to exploit the mechanism to promote and secure their own special interests. The diffusion of cultural values naturally adds to the number of such special interest groups. One consequence of the phenomenon of cultural diffusion, which is most prominent in liberal democratic societies, is the appearance of so-called "single-issue pressure groups", each of which has a strong commitment to promoting one particular position on a single social issue. As the number of such single-issue pressure groups multiplies, so does the number of problems over which the government is called on to make decisions. The decision-making process can get quite animated as these single-issue pressure groups tend to be unaccommodating towards positions other than their own.

The decision overload and the resulting immobility of the government naturally contribute to the sense of frustration the people feel about the effectiveness of their representative government in resolving social conflicts. The sense of frustration turns into anger when the government shows reluctance to make decisions for fear that any decision will surely antagonize some groups of individuals who will express strong opposition to it. Since maximizing the chance of reelection is a strong motive, as Downs has pointed out, on the part of elected officials, the government tends to opt for a status quo policy rather than a radical reform in social affairs (Downs [1957]). It is not surprising, then, if many people have begun to wonder if anything socially beneficial will ever come out of the democratic process of decision making.

In addition to the reluctance on the part of the government to take drastic policy measures, the influence the government has over the course of social affairs has also dwindled, especially in the area of macroeconomic policy. The insight of J.M. Keynes that the government can guide the performance of the national economy has come to be questioned in recent years as many governments have experienced the failure of their stabilization policies (Keynes [1936]). The effectiveness of a macroeconomic policy depends very much on how the private sector responds to the government's policy initiative. To the extent that the private sector tries to anticipate what the government is up to, the outcome of a policy could be very different from the one originally intended. Further, the degree to which economies of the world have become interdependent adds elements of uncertainty in the way the national economy behaves.

These are just a few symptoms of the dysfunction of democracy which we observe in the world today. Whether the whole situation deserves to be characterized as a crisis, more and more people are expressing their concern that the government, instead of promoting the general interests of the people, caters to the special interests of a small number of pressure groups on any social issue. If the knowledge explosion is indeed what has happened, it is clear that knowledge is not being translated into an effective execution of the democratic process of decision-making. This is the reason why the question of knowledge and power for democracy deserves a serious reexamination today.

A Taxonomy of Dysfunction

Democracy is a social arrangement in which the sovereign power lies with the people. If the people are to exercise their sovereign power effectively, it is essential that they possess knowledge of the things over which they are asked to make decisions. However, the people's capacity for knowledge cannot be taken for granted if the body of knowledge keeps on expanding as it has been in the last few centuries. As modern societies have come to depend more and more on the fruits of science and technology in organizing all aspects of social life, the range of social issues over which the people are called on to make decisions has dramatically expanded to reflect an exponential growth in the body of our scientific and technical knowledge.

Scientific and technical knowledge, to be sure, can be learned and disseminated by education. However, as the pursuit of science has become a highly specialized social activity, learning and dissemination of scientific and technical knowledge have become over and beyond what can be covered by general education. With the degree of specialization as advanced as it is today, it is almost impossible for any individual to absorb even the basics of a single scientific discipline without an extended period of professional training. The dilemma we face in a democratic society is that any social issue to be settled by the democratic decision-making process requires the counsel of so-called experts in one discipline—even several disciplines—deemed relevant to the issue at stake. Since experts can only go so far in clarifying the technical points of the issue even when they speak with one voice (which is not usually the case), the decision on any complicated social issue—whether it be an environmental issue or an economic one—may well be made out of ignorance on the part of the general public.

This type of dysfunction of democracy may be termed the "type-C" dysfunction—so termed after Coriolanus, a haughty Roman general in a Shakespeare play who, because of his aristocratic contempt for the wisdom of the masses, characterizes democracy as a system where "gentry, title, wisdom cannot conclude but by yea and no of general ignorance." This is a truly pathological case of the dysfunction because, after all, decisions are made in accordance with the democratic principle of implementing the will of the people. However, the will of the people in this case can hardly be called an informed judgment.

Whether decisions are made out of ignorance or reflect informed deliberation, no social action is exempt from the possibility that its consequences could be very different from the intended ones. This type of dysfunction may be termed the "type-M" dysfunction after Robert K. Merton, a sociologist who called our attention to the importance of unintended consequences of purposeful actions in social life (Merton [1957]). It is a dysfunction in that another action is needed if the outcome originally intended is to be regained, resulting in some cases in an endless cycle of action and corrective action. The possibility of the type-M dysfunction exists in a democratic society because the government, more often than not, fails to anticipate the people's reaction to its action. Thus, a tax cut intended to stimulate consumption may fail to bring about an increase in consumption if the consumers perceive it as just a temporary tax cut and not a permanent one. In addition to such errors in forecasting on the part of the government, unexpected changes in the environment can also trigger a type-M dysfunction. These unexpected changes range from weather to policies of foreign governments.

One important consequence of man being a social animal is that people tend to form groups and associations to pursue and promote their diverse goals and interests. Moreover, in societies where the democratic right of the freedom of association is granted, the number of these groups and associations tends to multiply as people's interests diversify. And as this process continues, the functioning of the whole society, including that of the representative government, comes into conflict with the functioning of groups and associations which are subsystems of society. The resulting loss of effectiveness of social action may be termed the "type-R" dysfunction, for it was Rousseau who foresaw this possibility for democratic societies. The majority rule ceases to be an effective method of reaching a social decision because "there are no longer as many votes as there are men but only as many votes as there are groups" (Rousseau [1968], p.73).

The phenomenon commonly referred to as "the power diffusion" is one manifestation of the type-R dysfunction. Note, however, that power diffusion is an essential, systemic feature of a democratic society as reflected, for example, in the separation of power among the executive, legislative and judiciary branches of the government. While intended as a device to maintain checks and balances among the three branches, the separation of power can lead to a stalemate, even an inconsistency, in the social decision-making process. The presence of political parties with widely different ideological orientations also contributes to the type-R dysfunction. And the phenomenon of cultural diffusion leads to a perverse case of the type-R dysfunction as the number of single-issue and other special interest groups multiplies, resulting in decision overload for the government.

Society is a complicated system as systems go and the complexity of the system gives rise to a dysfunction which reflects an inconsistency between different levels of the system. Consider, for example, the classic problem of organizing an economic system based on the individual pursuit of self-interest. Adam Smith saw no problem of level-inconsistency as long as the overall system called a market economy is organized on the principle of free competition (Smith [1937]). The problem of level-inconsistency is inevitable, however, since the pursuit of self-interest by individuals runs against the interests of the overall system to preserve limited resources. This is the situation described by Garrett Hardin in his "the tragedy of the commons" and may, therefore, be termed the "type-H" dysfunction (Hardin [1968]). A type-H dysfunction arises whenever the democratic principle of guaranteeing the freedom of individual activity leads to a conflict between the common interests of society and the private interests of individuals. The type-H dysfunction presents a special challenge for democratic societies because the common interests are not usually represented by any subsystem and, therefore, tend to be left unattended.

Knowledge, Power and Democracy

Of the four types of dysfunction which inflict democratic societies, only the type-C dysfunction explicitly refers to a lack of knowledge as the cause of dysfunction. However, the question of knowledge is inherent in all four types of dysfunction, each type representing a different sense in which knowledge is the source of power for the people.

Considering the complexity of social issues on which they are asked to make decisions today, it is unrealistic to assume that the people be informed of all the scientific and technical implications of these issues. Nevertheless, it is important that the people in a democratic society be at least knowledgeable about what science is all about. In particular, the people must be informed about the exploratory nature of all scientific inquiries, involving hypothesis-building and empirical verification, and the tentative nature of all scientific explanations which nevertheless command acceptance until they are replaced by better ones (Kuhn [1970]).

Knowing this much about science is a minimum requirement of responsible citizens in a democratic society if they are to make a judicious decision on a social issue based on expert opinions. It will also help them to understand why experts, even from a single discipline, do not necessarily speak with one voice. Having some knowledge about what it is that they are voting on is of crucial importance if the people are to possess some sense of control over the course of social events which affect their individual lives. There is indeed no magical cure for the type-C dysfunction except, as James Madison would say, for the people to arm themselves with the power which knowledge gives.

Uncertainty is an inherent feature of all human affairs and scientific predictions cannot go very far beyond extrapolations of certain statistical regularities culled from the accumulation of past observations. Since all predictions depend on the assumption that other things remain the same and, in reality, other things do not remain the same, no social action is exempt from having unintended consequences.

One reason why other things do not remain constant in social life is because a society operates in a space of eco-systemic interaction with other societies in all areas of human activity from foreign policy to international trade to cultural exchange. As such, the evolution of a social system is basically a stochastic process subject to random shocks and disturbances. In this sense, every society—democratic or otherwise—is susceptible to the type-M dysfunction. If a democratic society is to be wary of this type of dysfunction, it is because the type-M dysfunction at the level of individuals sometimes tends to be magnified into a major dysfunction at the aggregate level. Knowing this does not necessarily translate into concrete power, except perhaps to those who are lucky enough to make economic profits in the statistical game of market speculation. If knowledge translates into power in this instance, it is therefore power of a psychological kind which enables individuals to be prepared for the unexpected and unintended consequences of any social action.

The type-R dysfunction results from a simple mathematical fact that the number of all possible associations of individuals in a society is greater than the number of individuals in that society, i.e., $2^n > n$, where n is the number of individuals. Thus, the representative government, which is supposed to speak for the whole group, is no match against the complexity of groups and associations which advocate their own sets of values and follow their own rules of conduct. Unless all these groups and associations operate within a uniform frame of reference such as the Constitution, there is no way that the government can accommodate all the demands coming from different groups and associations. As is indeed clear with the case of religious freedom, a democratic society is not in a position to impose any uniform frame of reference in certain matters. The separation of church and state is no doubt a commendable posture in terms of guaranteeing the freedom of conscience but a sure way of inviting a type-R dysfunction.

Paradoxical as it may sound, the separation of power among three branches of government, which certainly contributes to the type-R dysfunction, serves at the same time as a cure for the same dysfunction as long as all three branches can be made to work for a uniform set of national interests. When too much power is concentrated in the executive branch, the government is very easily turned into a patron of a small number of individuals, groups and associations. When this happens, the prospect of having to face the voters in the next election becomes the only effective measure of rectifying the misrepresentation of the will of the people. The fact that all elected officials in a democratic society must face the verdict of the voting public is the sense in which knowledge can be the source of power in this instance. This knowledge is important because it can potentially restrain the tendency of the people to overexercise their democratic rights to promote their special interests by forming groups and associations.

The type-H dysfunction is of a systemic nature in that it is a reflection of an incongruence between the whole and the parts of a system. Even if all individual subsystems are operating in ways they are supposed to, there is no guarantee that the whole system will function in a manner which will promote the common interests, as is clear in the cases involving externalities or interdependence.

A democratic society typically tries to deal with the type-H dysfunction by setting up a public agency of one sort or another. The Environmental Protection Agency is one example of such a public agency whose task is to alleviate, if not cure, the tragedy of the commons. However, even a public agency of this sort is susceptible to the type-R dysfunction as it must deal with lobbying activities staged by such diverse interest groups as the oil industry, cattle ranchers, farmers, and hiking enthusiasts.

In logic the type-H dysfunction is known as the fallacy of composition. The type-H dysfunction is one reason why we often have separate, mutually inconsistent norms of behavior for individuals and for society. Thus, the killing of other human beings, which is punishable by law at the individual level, goes unpunished—indeed it is even glorified in some cases—at the national level.

If knowledge is to translate into power in this last instance, it must come from an awareness of an eco-systemic nature of our existence at both the individual and the aggregate level. Individuals are themselves subsystems of a larger system called society which operates with a set of rules and regulations intended to regulate individual behavior. Society, in turn, exists in the space of eco-systemic interaction with other societies which operate with their own sets of rules and regulations. And all human societies exist in the space of interaction with the system called "nature". However, since no individual, or society for that matter, is likely to speak for nature, we humans are, in a way, destined to be subject to the type-H dysfunction in our relation to the natural environment.

Conclusion

Given that democracy suffers from various types of dysfunction today, some may wonder whether a democratic form of government is just one phase in human history which is destined to be replaced by some other form of government. After all, it was Plato who warned of the possibility that democracy may pass into despotism. Others may be concerned about the fact that democratic societies represent a minority on the global scene and wonder whether democracy is an endangered species in the eco-system of human societies.

The fact of the matter is that democracy, like any other social system, does not offer a complete solution to the problem of organizing social life. Though incomplete, democracy does offer the best hope for the betterment of the human condition as it permits the people to be the master of their affairs not only in the political arena but also in the cultural and economic arenas. However, to the extent that democracy suffers from various types of dysfunction today, some institutional reforms may be necessary. For example, there is little doubt that the whole machinery of the government has to be simplified if the government is to become more responsive to the needs of the people. One way to accomplish this would be to restore the autonomy of local governments which will also have the benefit of regaining the people's sense of participation in the democratic decision-making process. Another would be to reduce the size of professional bureaucrats in favor of private citizens sitting on ad hoc commissions and committees to deal with the type-R dysfunction (Toffler [1980]).

No amount of institutional reform would rid democracy of dysfunction unless the people begin to exercise their sovereignty with full understanding of the sense in which knowledge is the source of power for them. And knowledge, which is so crucial for the functioning of democracy, must ultimately include a knowledge of Self (Unger [1975]). For unless each individual cultivates Self, knowledge would not lead to order but to chaos as he will seek his own special interests based on his own narrow view of the world. Although the spirit of diversity is the spirit of democracy, the diversity of human actions will not lead to order at the aggregate level unless each individual is guided by an awareness of his existence as an individual and a species. As a system built on imperfect beings called humans, knowledge of this dual nature of man's existence as an individual and as a species is the thread of life which sustains democracy as an effective form of organizing social life.

PART THREE

BALANCE AND COHERENCE IN
SOCIAL DEVELOPMENT

7. ECONOMIC DEVELOPMENT AS A
CYBERNETIC PROCESS

Introduction

Economic development, as those who have studied it readily concede, is more than just an economic phenomenon. It is a process of transformation for both society and the individuals in it, involving changes in economic, political and cultural institutions as well as in individual consciousness, attitudes and values. Some aspects of these changes can no doubt be, and have in fact been, formulated into theoretical models using such key economic aggregates as the gross national product, the capital stock and the savings ratio. However, since economic development is a process of transformation—the "Great Transformation", for that matter, as Karl Polanyi put it while describing the British experience—these theoretical models have not been successful in capturing all those unruly, non-economic factors such as climate, entrepreneurship and the work ethic which many students of economic development regard as important (Polanyi [1957]). Indeed, when it comes to the subject of economic development, one is tempted to reverse what Goethe said about theory and real life, for what is grey in this instance is not theory but the reality of life in the less developed countries (LDCs).

Some members of the LDCs, to be sure, have broken away from the doldrums of underdevelopment in recent years. But even in these cases it is not at all clear how much of their success owes to economic factors. In fact, the success of the newly industrialized nations (NICs), especially those four "dragons" in Asia, seems to offer a confirmation of the old thesis that economic development requires concerted endeavor of the whole nation in economic as well as other realms of human activity. As Fernand Braudel observes, "capitalism cannot be extricated from the society in which it is embedded; money, government, culture confront one another but support one another all the same" (Braudel [1980], p.110). While theoretical models have succeeded in highlighting the role of such economic factors as savings, investment in human capital, and research and development, dichotomizing economic and non-economic factors does not facilitate our understanding of economic development as one aspect of social change.

If we are to understand economic development as a process of social change and transformation, we must introduce a systems perspective which views economy as one part of the social system. This is done only by viewing society as a system consisting of the full diversity of human actions as these actions take place in diverse realms of social life. Only by developing such a systems frame-work will we be able to explain why some countries are trapped in the vicious cycle of underdevelopment while others have successfully taken off on their way to development. The need for a systems perspective actually goes beyond the need for a better insight into the phenomenon of economic development. A systems perspective is crucial for developing a sound basis for public policy, especially in view of the possibility that undesirable consequences of a policy must later be rectified by another policy.

Society as a System

In what sense is society a system? Before the advent of systems concepts and theories, there used to be two contending ideas on this question. On the one hand, there is the idea, fostered by the nominalist tradition, that society is a nominal entity defined simply as the sum of individuals, who are the only real entities. Society is basically a contrivance whose goal is to promote and coordinate the wishes and desires of individuals. The individual, moreover, is seen as an autonomous being, endowed with free will and rationality. This tradition, nurtur-ing the development of liberal democratic ideas and values, has provided impetus for the modernization of industrial nations in the West. The realist tradition, on the other hand, subscribes to the idea that society is something real and larger than the sum of individuals in it. In what sense society is a real entity has been given different shades of interpretation from Hobbes' conception of state as "Leviathan" to George Orwell's depiction of government as "Big Brother". Once the state is viewed as a real entity, there is a danger that it will be employed as a symbolic means of controlling and manipulating individual lives, as has indeed happened in countries such as Germany, Italy, and Japan in this century.

With the development of systems concepts and theories in this century, we have gained further insights into the way society functions as a system. What we propose to do here is to incorporate some of these insights to develop a more operational conception of society than the two polar conceptions as represented by the nominalist and realist traditions. To be more specific, we introduce a set of basic ideas about society which will together form what Popper calls a "metaphysical research programme" for the social sciences and which can therefore be used to analyze the phenomenon of social change in general and economic development in particular (Popper [1982]).

We begin with the idea that society is a system which is defined in the space of social actions:

Postulate I: Society is a system which exists in the space of all social actions as such actions take place in the three realms of *'culture', 'economy'* and *'polity'*.

By "culture" we mean the set of all social actions pertaining to the creation and dissemination of ideas, values and symbols, by "economy" the set of all social actions pertaining to the production and distribution of goods and services, and by "polity" the set of all actions pertaining to the maintenance of justice and social order. These subsystems of "culture", "economy" and "polity" are introduced as the frames of reference for different types of social actions and need not define distinct and disjoint sets. As a matter of fact, the course of evolution of a social system is very much determined by the manner in which these three subsystems overlap and interact with one another.

As society is seen here as consisting of three broad subsystems of culture, economy and polity, the state of society as a whole can be represented by an "ensemble" of information with vectors of appropriate dimensions chosen to represent these three subsystems:

> ***Postulate II:*** The state of a social system at any given time can be repre-
> sented by the social process vector which contains an ensemble of social
> information.

With this postulate, the course of evolution of a social system can be represented by the social process vector $\{x_{(t)}, y_{(t)}, z_{(t)}; t \varepsilon T\}$, where $x_{(t)}$ stands for the vector for the cultural process, $y_{(t)}$ for the vector for the economic process, and $z_{(t)}$ for the vector for the political process. This is the framework we employ in analyzing social change in general which engulfs all of the cultural, economic and political subsystems. This is, therefore, the framework we employ in analyzing economic development as it properly represents economic change as one aspect of social change. Since "economy" is embedded in an overall system called "society", isolating the phenomenon of economic development from social change in general provides us a partial—and perhaps deceptive—information about the nature of social change taking place within a given society. Our framework overcomes this difficulty by paying attention to systemic interactions of economy with other social subsystems which will be reflected on the way the "observed" social process vectors behave over time.

There are certain systemic features of the underlying social system which need to be reflected as the revealed characteristics of the social process if our analysis is to be fruitfully employed in explaining economic development. First, the social process, because of the complexity of the patterns of social interactions within and across societies, is not reducible to a deterministic process and must therefore be seen as a stochastic process:

> ***Postulate III:*** The social process is a stochastic process.

Although the social process is a stochastic process, it is subject to certain drift as well as some degree of control and management because it represents the evolution of a social as opposed to a natural system. This idea is captured in the next postulate:

> ***Postulate IV:*** Every component process of the social process is subject
> to transmutation from past social actions taken in that and other realms.

The role of the Protestant ethic in the development of capitalist economies, as discussed by Tawney and Max Weber, is an outstanding example of a transmutation of the social process in which economic actions are affected by the values acquired in the past in the cultural realm (Tawney [1926], Weber [1930]). Transmutations may also take the form of economic events influencing the cultural process.

Finally, we specify the sense in which the social process is a cybernetic process. When we speak of the social process being a cybernetic process, we are only using this term to suggest the possibility that society can be subjected to some degree of steering, as is discussed by Cornelis, via communication of socially useful information among societal members (Cornelis [1990]). Needless to say, the subsystem that does the steering is the political subsystem:

Postulate V: Society is a cybernetic system in the sense that its evolution is subject to steering by the political subsystem.

The degree to which the government is successful in steering will be different from one society to another and from one time to another even for the same society. From a formal point of view, these differences can be represented by the differences in the dimension of the social process vector affected by government actions.

Economic Development as a Cybernetic Process

The standard treatment of economic development treats economic development mainly as an economic phenomenon. Such separation of economy from culture and other realms of human activity is a modern phenomenon which has become pronounced with the expansion of market economies. However, even in societies where the logic of the marketplace dictates social actions, the individuals manage to find outlets for the exchange of cultural values, symbols and ideas in their economic transactions. The upshot is the coexistence, in all capitalist societies, of the market economy on the one hand and what Braudel terms "the economics of everyday life" on the other (Braudel [1979]). This suggests a rather subtle manner in which culture and economy interact in the evolution of a social system.

The influence of culture is also observed in the phenomenon of the work ethic which some societies seem to possess more than others. In addition to the work ethic, we also need to pay attention to such cultural factors as entrepreneurship, which Schumpeter regards as the key feature of capitalist economic development, and the leadership quality of politicians who formulate economic policies (Schumpeter [1949]). What is at issue here is what type of society engenders the kinds of psychological motivations and personality orientations which promote economic development.

An episode in modern Chinese history known as the Cultural Revolution serves to illustrate the somewhat uneasy relationship among culture, economy and polity which often conflict with one another before they can be unified into a concerted national effort for economic development. When, in 1966, Mao Zedong introduced the "Sixteen Points Programme" to kick off the Cultural Revolution, it was his intention to improve the performance of the economy by bringing about changes in the people's consciousness and value system. What Mao recognized in China at the time was the need for "an education to develop morally, intellectually and physically and to become laborers with socialist consciousness and culture". If the Cultural Revolution failed to reform the consciousness of the Chinese people, this episode illustrates the importance of viewing society as a cybernetic system: Even with the strong political leadership of the Communist party, those policies which were embedded in the Sixteen Points Programme failed to expand the space of cultural and economic actions spanned by these policies.

This example also illustrates the strategic importance of developing a communications network as a basis for social steering which is needed for economic development. Money is, of course, the universal symbol of communication in the economic subsystem. It facilitates market transactions because it communicates exchange values of goods and services to the market participants.

However, money can very easily be converted into a symbol of social achievement as well as a means of gaining access to and exercising political power. Some degree of prestige accorded to business activity is no doubt needed for economic development which, as many observers have pointed out, is lacking in the LDCs. What Japan experienced at the time of the Meiji Restoration well illustrates this point. For the undoing of the Tokugawa Shogunate was the result as much of its failure to recognize the importance of harnessing and managing the acquisitive drive of the merchants as of its failure to cope with the pressure exerted by foreign powers to open up the country and modernize the political system. By imposing an artificial political order which placed the merchant class at the bottom of the social ladder, the Shogunate invited the rebellion of the lower samurai who saw the advantage of allying with the merchant class in promoting their cause of political reform. Having gained political power with the Restoration, these lower samurai helped unleash the acquisitive drive of merchants and industrialists who were now united in the goal of promoting the national interest in their private business ventures.

These examples serve to illustrate the importance of a systems perspective in understanding the phenomenon of economic development. This is the reason why we propose to view economic development as a cybernetic process, for a social system needs to be steered if it is to establish coordination and cooperation of its component subsystems. The evolution of a social system involves shifting patterns of connections among, and varying degrees of transformations of, these component subsystems.

When the term "cybernetics" is applied to social systems, its meaning must be flexibly interpreted. As Maruyama points out, a social system is, more often than not, a deviation-amplifying mutual causal system (Maruyama [1960]). This explains why coordination and cooperation of component social subsystems are crucial for economic development. Consider, for example, the problem of entrepreneurship in the LDCs. Besides the obvious psychological and cultural factors, the LDCs also lack political and structural support for the cultivation and fostering of entrepreneurship. Moreover, all these negative factors reinforce one another, trapping in this case these LDCs in the vicious cycle of underdevelopment. For one thing, the governments in the LDCs often restrict the growth of entrepreneurs from ethnic and communal groups other than those who have direct ties with the country's political leaders. Even when these people overcome political restrictions, their efforts are frustrated by the underdevelopment of capital markets, which makes business ventures more risky and uncertain than otherwise. To be sure, some wealthy families with strong ties with the political leadership have emerged in some LDCs with their operations extending into several industries. Even here the monopolistic control these families exercise creates market distortions which have serious consequences on the distribution of income and the spread of entrepreneurship. The lack of entrepreneurship is not, therefore, by itself a serious hindrance to economic development for the LDCs. Rather, it is the lack of coordination and cooperation of all the relevant factors in all of the cultural, economic and political subsystems that shackles the LDCs. It is therefore the failure of the whole system, not of this or that factor in a specific subsystem, that traps the LDCs in the vicious cycle of underdevelopment.

Conclusion

Economic development as one aspect of social change is tied inseparably with the historical development of the society in question. This points to the importance of collective memory and learning on the part of the whole population. While changes in social organizations and institutions can be brought about in relatively short periods of time, changes in people's consciousness tend to be rather slow, taking decades—even centuries—before concrete changes are noticed in the surface structure of the social system. Recall, for example, how long it took for the Protestant West to take off on its way to industrialization and economic development after the Reformation. Or, for that matter, consider the case of Japan where the people still carry on their affairs with their long-cherished values and norms even after they have supposedly accomplished their task of modernizing their country. If these are any indications, it is difficult to be optimistic about the prospect for changes in the people's consciousness in the LDCs.

The difficult task the LDCs face in bringing about the kind of social transformation needed for economic development is made complicated by the uncertainties of the world economic system. Some LDCs have been brought into the precarious position of dependency on the advanced industrial countries by their former colonial masters. For others their uncertain dependency stems from a lack of exports other than a few raw materials or of domestic financial institutions which would foster the development of indigenous entrepreneurship. When the world is seen as a social system, we are witnessing a rather fragile cybernetic system which lacks "organic coherence", bound together by the network of economic transactions but separated by cultural differences and political constraints. While the advanced industrialized countries carry on their international trade with their homage to the ideas of the Philosophical Radicals who saw in the logic of the marketplace a unifying principle which would transcend cultural and political barriers, the rest of the world struggles to stem the tide of economic advances coming from these countries in its efforts to preserve cultural identity and political autonomy. Since no single effective decider oversees the course of evolution of the world system as a cybernetic process, the LDCs are burdened by the uncertain future they face not only in their own countries but also in other parts of the world.

8. COORDINATING SOCIAL AND TECHNOLOGICAL DEVELOPMENT

Introduction

The problem of coordinating social and technological development is as old as human history as every society had to depend on technology as a means of sustaining life. In fact, dependence on technology is every bit as human as our quest for spiritual truth which has given us our religions and philosophical systems. While technology has expanded our faculties and enhanced our standard of living, we have come to learn at the same time that technology can be misused to disrupt social life and can indeed destroy all forms of life on this planet. Even those who do not share such a pessimistic outlook on technology are now ready to express their doubt on the value of technological development for the sake of technological development.

A feeling that technological development may have gone too far and out of our control is expressed with increasing frequency in public speeches, scholarly treatises and works of art. Many believe that technology has acquired its own law of progress, its own notion of rationality and its own set of values which can no longer be managed, let alone controlled, by an individual, by an organization, or even by a nation. Some go as far as characterizing the predicament we find ourselves in as the crisis of the technological society, for we seem to be driven by the technological imperative society imposes on us.

Many symptoms can indeed be detected to support the claim that our kind of technological society now faces a serious crisis. Some of these symptoms pertain to individuals, others to organizations, and still others to society as a whole. The individual faces a crisis of human development as the technological imperative not only propels the fragmentation of his work, thus depriving him of the opportunity to experience work as an integral part of his life, but also places his work in constant danger of being replaced by a machine of ever-sophisticated capacity. Organizations in the technological society struggle with the rigidity of their bureaucratic structure which they have developed to take full advantage of the mechanization of production processes. Society as a whole suffers from asymmetry between social and technological development, for the logic of technological development leaves little room for cultural tradition and human emotions.

These and other symptoms of the crisis of the technological society are also symptoms of the crisis of a civilization which has guided human evolution for the last couple of centuries since the advent of industrial societies. If we are to prevent the crisis from escalating itself into a disaster for our species, we must at least begin our effort to try to comprehend the nature of this crisis. As we correctly diagnose the nature of the crisis, we can redirect our effort to formulating social policies that will restore the balance between social and technological development which is sadly missing in the technological society today.

Diagnosing the Crisis of the Technological Society

What is the nature of the crisis that engulfs the technological society today, whose symptoms are observed at the level of individuals, of organizations, and of society as a whole? The loss of wholeness and the diffusion of identity the individual suffers in the technological society may be diagnosed to be the symptoms of the type-D disorder. The fragmentation of the life process the individual suffers in the technological society is one consequence of modernization which has been guided by the world-view originally formulated by Descartes. In its stylized form, the Cartesian world-view treats the world as consisting of the sum of non-interacting parts and components (Koizumi [1990]). The notion of rationality implied by this world-view is that an organization operates most effectively and efficiently when a given operation is decomposed into smaller and standardized tasks. Each individual is thus assigned a small fraction of the whole operation, rarely given an opportunity to experience work as an integral part of the life process. The fragmentation of the life process naturally leads to the fragmentation of personality because the demands of the workplace force the individual to develop what Jung called *persona*, a mask which the individual wears to cover up his true self (Jung [1969]).

The professionalization of various jobs and occupations is a necessary outcome of the Cartesian notion of rationality. While professionalizing a job or an occupation has some advantage in raising productivity and promoting the solidarity of an occupation, it develops into a disorder when the resulting rigidity hinders the coordination of tasks to be performed by people in different occupations. And the coordination of tasks performed by people in different occupations has become extremely important in our kind of technological society characterized by the division of labor and the segmentation of operation.

The type of disorder which afflicts organizations in the technological society may be termed the type-W disorder. While the type-D disorder results from a rigid application of the Cartesian notion of retionality to the division of labor among individuals, the type-W disorder reflects a malfunction in the vertical integration of an organization. We call this type of malfunction the type-W disorder because it was Max Weber who recognized a tendency towards bureaucratization as one important aspect of modernization (Weber [1978]). The bureaucratization of an organization evolves from the application of a notion of rationality that an organization can best be managed by a hierarchic system of control over its operation which involves finely classified subdivisions of different tasks to be performed by many individuals.

In the economic arena, the Weberian notion of rationality was promoted vigorously in the early part of this century under the name of Taylorism, or scientific management (Taylor [1911]). Scientific management of economic organizations with a hierarchic system of control led to the rise of large corporations whose operation needed a system of management other than a voluntary cooperation among participants. And as the size of economic organizations expanded, the size of bureaucracy in the political arena had to expand with it. For it became increasingly clear that polity in industrial society had to manage the economy effectively if it was to live up to its commitment to promoting the material well-being of its citizens.

Individuals and organizations develop symptoms of disorder because the society in which they live and operate, through its laws and institutions, encourages and promotes a specific notion of rationality and a specific set of values. The notion of rationality and the set of values which the technological society encourages and promotes are at the root of the third type of disorder. It will be termed the type-C disorder after Chung Tzu, or Master Chung as he is popularly called by the Chinese (Needham [1969]).

Chung Tzu distinguished among three aspects of technology. First, there is the mechanical aspect of technology which shows us how things work. Second, there is the practical aspect of technology which enables us to do things for us. Chung Tzu then went on to discuss the third aspect of technology which has to do with our mental dependency on technology. Since technology shows us how things work and enables us to do things for us, we are too apt to develop a mental dependency on technology which is soon converted into a faith in the power of technology—a faith that, whenever there is a problem, there is always a technical solution.

In the technological society, the whole social system is designed to encourage and promote technical solutions—widely interpreted to include applications of the human and social sciences—to social problems. As a result, the notion of rationality, which is relevant to technological development, is applied to even those social problems which require ethical and moral considerations. Hardin drew our attention to the type-C disorder inherent in the technological society by showing the existence of a class of problems for which there are no technical solutions (Hardin [1968]).

The crisis of the technological society is thus a reflection of an asymmetry between social and technological development. While technological development constantly ushers in new ways of doing things, social development is engaged in an almost hopeless struggle to manage social change triggered by the introduction of new technologies. In the sense that the crisis of the technological society is caused by the pace of technological development which has become too fast for society—and the individuals in it—to adapt to, modern technology, as Mumford correctly pointed out, is anti-social, following its own laws of progress which often disrupt the inertia built into social development in the form of cultural heritage and historical tradition (Mumford [1963]). Individuals in the technological society are constantly forced to adapt to technological development instead of having technology developed to meet their needs in human development.

Coordinating Social and Technological Development

The imbalance between social and technological development, which is tilted so dramatically to the side of technology today, is undermining the viability and cohesion of the technological society as a social system. If the crisis is to be duly dealt with, restoring symmetry between social and technological development is thus an urgent task of social institutions—politicians, social scientists and, of course, technologists.

As in other matters, history provides us useful guidance in this task as well. Our first task here is, therefore, to examine how different societies have traditionally dealt with the problem of coordinating social and technological development. Seeking insight from history is essential if we are to avoid the mistake which we, as George Santayana reminds us, are too apt to make for our myopia.

The Greeks dealt with the problem of coordinating social and technological development by their adherence to the conception of life which emphasized balance and harmony. Maintaining balance and harmony in all things prevented the Greeks from falling victim to the type-D disorder. The type-W disorder was not a major problem for the Greeks as long as the household remained the dominant form of social organization, for the household did not require a hierarchic system of control except in its dealings with the slaves. The Greeks were able to avoid the pitfall of the type-C disorder because, to them, science and technology represented two separate types of human activities. In fact, as Ellul points out, the cultivation of technology was regarded as inferior to the pursuit of science (Ellul [1964]). The Greek solution to the problem of coordinating social and technological development, from a social systems perspective, was thus based on the primacy of culture over economy.

The Chinese, in contrast, depended on the primacy of polity over culture and economy in their treatment of the problem of coordinating social and technological development. In a way, it was a Weberian control of the social process by the bureaucracy which the Chinese had perfected before the advent of modern bureaucratic states. The Chinese solution is interesting in that their bureaucrats were "literati", or men of letters, who did not consider technology as an essential tool for social control. Polity run by "cultured" bureaucrats and economy based on peasant farming prevented the Chinese from accomplishing an industrial revolution, though they had made remarkable technological innovations which would certainly have contributed to the industrialization of that society had they chosen to do so (Needham [1969]).

The Industrial Revolution, as is widely recognized, is a seminal event in the evolution of technological civilization which has given birth to modern industrial societies. We call the way in which industrial societies have been dealing with the problem of coordinating social and technological development the Anglo-

American solution, for the Industrial Revolution was very much a British revolution whose spirit has been enthusiastically endorsed and vigorously promoted by the Americans for the last century or so.

The main feature of the Anglo-American solution is that economy retains relative autonomy from polity in that the market mechanism is used to regulate the excesses of self-interest. There is also an interesting alliance of culture and economy, of science and technology, in modern industrial societies. For the first time in human history, we see the commercial interest as a motivating factor in technological development which relies heavily on advances in basic science. It is because of the merging of economy and technology that modern technology has come to acquire what Capra calls the "masculine consciousness" such as aggression, expansion and exploitation, for the logic of the marketplace embodies these masculine values (Capra [1982]).

The anti-social and anti-environmental tendency of modern technology has been kept under control by the ever-expanding scope of government intervention and regulation of industrial activities. As long as economy was allowed a fair degree of autonomy, it was necessary to deal with the undesirable consequences of technological development by creating governmental agencies and ministries. Thus, as economy expanded, so did polity, resulting in a Weberian, if not an Orwellian, nightmare of a huge bureaucracy overseeing every aspect of social life.

Reviewing how the Greek, Chinese and Anglo-American societies have traditionally dealt with the problem of coordinating social and technological development is useful in deriving hints as to what needs to be done if we are to avert the crisis of the technological society. From a social systems perspective, the imbalance between social and technological development reflects a lack of organic coherence among the component subsystems of culture, economy and polity. To be more specific, the crisis of the technological society has developed mainly because the Anglo-American solution has become increasingly ineffective against the realities of technological development. In the Anglo-American solution, technology, allied with economy, predominates culture and polity, which are supposed to provide meaning and guidance to human development and societal evolution. This being the case, it is clear that we need to bring back some aspects of the Greek and Chinese solutions in the designing and reforming of our laws and institutions.

Social and Technological Development in Relation to Human Development

From a social systems perspective, each of the three solutions to the problem of coordinating social and technological development is defective in that each favors the dominance of one subsystem over the other subsystems. When society is conceived as existing in the space of interaction among culture, economy and polity, it is essential that there exist some kind of balance, or organic coherence, among these subsystems. Technological development, with its own laws of progress, tends to disturb this balance, undermining the coherence of a social system. Hence, it is left to social development to maintain the organic coherence of a social system. And social development, since technology is ubiquitous in the technological society, must involve designing and reforming all the laws and institutions in all of the cultural, economic and political spheres of social life.

Of vital importance to this task of social development is whether our laws and institutions can be made more accommodating to human development. The existing laws and institutions of the technological society are seriously flawed in this respect because technological development embodies "masculine consciousness" which encourages development of such values as competition, exploitation, segmentation and manipulation. If technology is to aid human development, it is obvious that we need to encourage the development of "feminine consciousness" which embodies such values as cooperation, nurture, integration and accommodation. It is not impossible to accomplish this task because human development, as a process which involves interaction among the biological, psychological and social aspects of the individual human existence, can be made to correspond to social development which takes place in the space of interaction among "nature", "culture" and "society".

The technological society, with its inherent bias towards technological development in societal evolution, tends to disturb the overall balance among the biological, social and psychological processes of human development. The industrial phase in the evolution of the technological society, in particular, has developed technologies which have had a destructive impact on nature, has introduced a centralized and hierarchic system of management and control in society, and has maintained an uneasy—sometimes antagonistic—relationship with culture (Bell [1976]). Why this has been the case is not difficult to see because the industrial society has systematically favored the development of "hard" technologies which embody masculine consciousness. In short, the social environment for human development in the technological society has not been a very hospitable one.

If the individual is to feel at home in the technological society, it is essential that technology serve the role of mediator, not manipulator, of the process of human development for each individual. In fact, this is the sense in which "technical education" is to be interpreted and administered. Technology, by its very nature, represents the disembodiment of a human faculty, be it of a manual or an intellectual kind. Once technology is disembodied, i.e., once technology establishes its existence as an exo-somatic entity, it acquires its own laws of development in societal evolution apart from the intentions and desires of those who develop technologies. This is indeed the reason why technological development can become inhuman, anti-social and anti-environmental. If technology is to serve the role of mediator of human development while maintaining balance with social development, technological development must not deprive the individual of the sense of affinity to technology, though it, of necessity, will lead a life of its own once detached from the human body.

Conclusion

Coordinating social and technological development has an important implication for democracy as a form of social system. In particular, retaining a sense of affinity to technology is essential if the individual is to retain a sense of belonging in the operation of social organizations. Since technology can be detached from the human body, its ownership can be concentrated in the hands of a few individuals and its users can then become subject to manipulation by these owners. And to the extent that technological development embodies the logic of linear expansion, it promotes the growth of bureaucracy in an effort to control and manage social organizations whose size tends to expand with technology. These possibilities suggest that technological development in the technological society can also be anti-democratic.

Restoring a sense of affinity to technology is important if we are to preserve democracy, which exhibits many symptoms of dysfunction today, as a viable form of social arrangement (Koizumi [1988]). Restoring a sense of affinity to technology is the first step towards restoring a sense of autonomy which the individual needs if he is to function as a responsible member of a participatory democracy. It will also enhance the individual's sense of belonging in the workplace, not as an antagonistic member of either labor or management but as a cooperative member of the operation of which he is an integral part.

Ideally, technology must be able to mediate the process of self-actualization for the individual. As society provides the context in which human development takes place, in a society where technology is exploitative and manipulative, the individual tends to develop these same qualities. The technological society has largely been a failure in terms of developing technologies which aid human development.

The "cybernetic" society which has emerged with the development of computers and other new cybernetic technologies in the last few decades offers some promise of creating a more hospitable environment for human development. However, whether the cybernetic society will turn out to be more accommodating to human development and, therefore, more conducive to the development of democratic social organizations will depend crucially on whether those who engage in technological development will do so with an awareness that technological development can be harmful—even devastating—to human development unless it maintains the organic coherence of society as a system. Indeed, no new technology will exempt us from the need to address ourselves to the problem of coordinating social and technological development.

9. NATIONALISM AS IDEOLOGY, NATIONALISM AS EMOTION, AND THE PITFALLS OF NATIONAL DEVELOPMENT

Introduction

There are two meanings to the term "nationalism". The term, on the one hand, refers to an ideology, a political theory, which expounds how a nation can serve as a unit of social life for individuals from diverse backgrounds. On the other, it refers to an emotion, a psychological bond, which unites a group of individuals. While nationalism as ideology regards a nation as an aggregate of citizens and thus defines nationality in terms of citizenship, nationalism as emotion treats a nation as the homeland for a group of individuals and defines nationality in terms of common historical experience or cultural heritage of these individuals.

The evolution of modern nation-states amply illustrates that these two meanings of nationalism—nationalism as ideology and nationalism as emotion—seldom, if ever, converge for a real-life nation. Whenever nationalism as ideology fails to maintain social cohesion for demographic, political or other reasons, the underlying tension between these two forms of nationalism surfaces as animosities, confrontations, and violent clashes among different national groups as each group starts to assert the legitimacy of its own version of nationalism as emotion.

National development is destined to be a bumpy ride over many pitfalls just because the tension between nationalism as ideology and nationalism as emotion is unavoidable. National development may be deemed "successful" to the extent that a nation is able to manage the tension between the two forms of nationalism in its evolution as a social system. This naturally raises the question of why national development has been successful only in certain parts of the world and not in others. This is one of the questions we hope to examine in this chapter.

There is another and more important question which needs to be examined. And this is the question of what is the extent to which national development can be strictly a national phenomenon. A turbulent history of national development in Eastern Europe since the end of World War II, for example, shows how easy it is for national development to be influenced by external events and forces. Indeed, no discussion of national development would be meaningful today unless it is done in the context of the network of global interdependence which now envelops all nations of the world.

Nationalism as Ideology versus Nationalism as Emotion

Nationalism as ideology grew out of a painful history of protest and revolt against the authoritarian control of the people by a small number of royalties and aristocrats (Armstrong [1982]). It has played an important role in the evolution of modern nation-states in Western Europe and the United States of America, thanks to the efforts of such thinkers as Rousseau and Michelet in France, Locke and Bagehot in England, Jefferson and Paine in America, and von Treischke in Germany. It has been effectively exploited to legitimize efforts to unify diverse social groups with diverse cultural and historical backgrounds and, during its heyday in the nineteenth century, even to assimilate foreign national groups (Russell [1962]).

The central tenet of nationalism as ideology is an assertion that individuals, endowed with certain inalienable rights, are the real actors of social life and thus form a nation in order to protect and promote these rights. It is not necessary, therefore, that different individuals be treated differently even though individuals carry their own individualities such as their ethnic background, cultural heritage, or religious faith. All it matters is that individuals carry common citizenship as the members of a nation which is defined as the unit of political life.

Nationalism as ideology is a radical doctrine. This explains why it emerged as an effective principle of organizing social life only in certain parts of the world where the people had built up such traditions as the separation of church and state, the legitimacy of the profit motive in the economy, and the acquisition of knowledge as an autonomous activity (Schopflin [1990]). Even in those countries where such traditions had been built up, it was necessary, as the historian James illustrates with his recent work on the German experience, to introduce nationalist movements of one sort or another—the adoption of national flags, the singing of national anthems, the construction of national museums, the celebration of national holidays, and so on—to foster national identity among citizens coming from diverse historical and cultural backgrounds (James [1990]). In other parts of the world where such traditions had not evolved, nationalism as ideology had to be complemented by the authoritarian control of the people by the government in order to maintain the cohesion of a nation.

What distinguishes nationalism as emotion from nationalism as ideology is a psychological sense of belonging which unifies a group of individuals as the members of a nation. This sense of belonging may be a result of these individuals sharing a common history. It may also be a reflection of their race, faith, geography, or language. As Joseph Stalin put it, "[a] nation is a historically evolved, stable community of language, territory, economic life and psychological make-up in a community of culture" (Hobsbawn [1990], p.112). Rooted as it is in "blood, soil, and tongue", nationalism as emotion appeals to the people's sense of loyalty to their homeland and fosters a national identity based on an emotional bond even among those who are forced to lead the life of exiles for one reason or another. It is not surprising, then, that nationalism as emotion has found its supporters among philosophers and artists with a Romantic inclination such as von Herder, Schiller and Smetana.

Nationalism as emotion, while it promotes a sense of solidarity among a group of individuals, is not effective as an organizing principle of social life for a modern complex nation consisting of diverse national groups. It seldom, if ever, coincides with nationalism as ideology, which defines nationality in terms of citizenship. While a nation as a community of citizens can be a home for diverse national groups, a nation as a community of individuals sharing a common culture tends to accord special privileges to one national group to the exclusion of other national groups who often feel neglected and marginalized in what they consider to be their own nation (Bendix [1964]).

Nationalism and National Development

Nationalism as ideology and nationalism as emotion have different implications for national development. This is so because national development, defined here as the evolution of a nation as a social system, follows different paths as the differences between the two forms of nationalism induce different patterns of interaction among culture, economy, and polity as the subsystems of a social system.

One way of looking at the differences between nationalism as ideology and nationalism as emotion for their implications for national development is in terms of the cohesion of a nation as a social system. A nation which is guided by nationalism as ideology can be characterized as what anthropologists call a low-context society in that social interactions there tend to be based on contractual relationships among autonomous individuals (Hall [1976]). In contrast, a nation which is guided by nationalism as emotion can be identified as a high-context society in that social interactions there tend to be influenced, if not determined, by kinship relations and personal connections. Needless to say, the cohesion of a nation as a social system tends to be more intense in a high-context society, to the extent that the people carry out their social transactions with the sense of sharing a common emotional bond. On the other hand, a high-context nation may tend to be ethnocentric and non-accommodating towards cultural values, languages and religions other than its own.

More directly relevant to the issue of national development, nationalism as ideology and nationalism as emotion tend to promote different values which guide individual behavior. To be specific, nationalism as ideology, with its constitutional guarantee of individual autonomy in social life, promotes such values as individuality, self-reliance, efficiency, and entrepreneurship. In contrast, nationalism as emotion, with its emphasis on shared heritage and experience, promotes such values as collectivism, cooperation, equity, and conservatism.

These differences in value orientations explain why in countries where nationalism as ideology has taken root the principle of market exchange based on contractual relationships predominates economic life, whereas in countries guided by nationalism as emotion the principle of "reciprocity" serves better as an organizing principle of economic life (Polanyi [1977]). Eastern European nations would face special difficulty in embracing and fostering market capitalism because in this part of Europe "the market principle is the alien body within the centralized, redistributive economy" (Hankiss [1990], p.199). In other words, in these nations the people have become accustomed to the principle of "reciprocity" as complemented by the channels of "redistribution" established by the government. In contrast, if nations in Western Europe and North America have generally been more successful in stimulating capital accumulation and technical progress, it is because these nations have fostered a tradition of maintaining autonomy in both commerce and science from secular as well as ecclesiastic authorities. In political life nationalism as ideology supports the idea of a representative government and bureaucracy based on individual merits while nationalism as emotion tends to support and perpetuate a paternalistic government and bureaucracy based on personal connections (Eisenstadt and Lemarchand [1981]).

	NATIONALISM AS IDEOLOGY	NATIONALISM AS EMOTION
NATION	A COMMUNITY OF CITIZENS SHARING A POLITICAL LIFE	A COMMUNITY OF PEOPLE WITH COMMON HERITAGE
NATIONALITY	CITIZENSHIP	SENTIMENT (Volksgeist)
SOCIAL INTERACTION	CONTRACT LOW-CONTEXT	CONNECTION HIGH-CONTEXT
INTEGRATION	FEDERATION	EMOTIONAL BOND
IDENTITY	SOCIALIZATION	HERITAGE
VALUE ORIENTATION	INDIVIDUALISM ACHIEVEMENT EFFICIENCY MERITOCRACY ENTREPRENEURSHIP	COLLECTIVISM STATUS EQUITY CLIENTELISM MUTUAL SUPPORT

There are important differences in the way national goals are formulated, implemented, and revised between those nations guided by nationalism as ideology and those guided by nationalism as emotion. To the extent that the goals of national development are formulated in nations guided by nationalism as ideology through the democratic decision-making process, they tend to transcend the agendas and desires of specific national groups, for the policies formulated by the central government must embody a certain degree of universalism if they are to apply to the whole nation. Here revisions and reformulations of national goals are unavoidable because various national groups will engage in lobbying activities to restore and/or promote their own specific agendas and desires. As it is impossible to incorporate all the agendas and desires of diverse national groups, national goals under nationalism as ideology tend to be subject to constant revisions and reformulations unless the central government can maintain strong leadership over an extended period of time.

The goals of national development in nations guided by nationalism as emotion would have the characteristics of more faithfully reflecting the sentiment of the people as the government officials and bureaucrats also come from the same national group. National goals tend to be more enduring, though they are not exempt from revisions and reformulations which need to be made as changes in cultural values and technologies take place. Revisions and reformulations of national goals also become necessary in response to changes taking place in other nations.

Of the literature on national development, modernization theory has prevailed among Western social scientists for a long time (Levy [1966]). Modernization theory in the context of our discussion would argue for the growing importance of nationalism as ideology as an organizing principle of social life for a modern complex nation. However, modernization theory has fared miserably in explaining, let alone predicting, modernization and economic development of non-Western nations. The reason why modernization theory has not been successful in explaining the development experience of non-Western nations is that it fails to pay enough attention to the presence of different principles behind national development in different nations.

Even when modernization is seen mainly in its economic aspect, the experience of East Asian nations such as Japan, Korea, Taiwan, Hong Kong, and Singapore is quite different from the experience of Western nations in that in these nations nationalism as emotion has worked as a complementary factor to nationalism as ideology. The situation has been quite different in Eastern Europe where nationalism as ideology has not evolved as a unifying principle of organizing social life and thus has been too weak to manage diverse calls for nationalism as emotion coming from diverse ethnic groups.

National Development in an Interdependent World

A nation as a social system is an open system. As such, no nation, whether guided by nationalism as ideology or nationalism as emotion, can hope to formulate and implement its goals of national development independently of its interactions with other nations. The task for a nation of maintaining its cohesion as a social system is made more difficult in an interdependent world because it must balance the goal of promoting national development against other goals such as the defense of the homeland, the protection of national interests in the global economy, and the preservation of national heritage and identity.

The preservation of national heritage and identity—customs, language, religion, and values—deserves special mention here because one aspect of global interdependence involves the adoption—voluntary or involuntary—of an ideology that transcends both nationalism as ideology and nationalism as emotion. For nearly fifty years since the end of World War II, much of Central and Eastern Europe has been under the spell of one such supra-national ideology called communism. Communism as ideology has tried, in the same way that nationalism as ideology has, to bring together diverse national groups with one sweeping ideology that transcends national borders. However, while nationalism as ideology has proved to be a workable principle of organizing social life founded as it is on a realistic assumption about human nature and social institutions, communism as ideology has turned out to be an unworkable principle as it was based, from the very beginning, on an unrealistic, utopian vision about human nature and social institutions. If communism has survived as long as it has in this part of Europe, it is because the cohesion of a nation as a social system has been tightly maintained by the authoritarian control of the central government.

The holding power of an ideology over a nation is limited only by the extent to which the central government is able to shield from the people the picture of greener pastures beyond the national border. The disappearance of communism from the landscape of Central and Eastern Europe adumbrates the difficulty nationalism as ideology will face before it can guide national development in this part of the world and elsewhere faced with similar challenges. For one thing, nationalism as ideology will have to accomplish the same task of transcending diverse national groups without the utopian myth and the authoritarian control of communism. Moreover, the appeal of greener pastures beyond the national border is here and now as life on the other side of the national border is vividly displayed on television screens. In other words, it would be very difficult for the people to accept that national development, like human development, requires time for maturation.

The problem of maturation for national development is complicated by the fact that different spheres of a social system require different maturational times. Of the three subsystems of culture, economy, and polity, the pace of change is fastest in the economic arena as it is here that investors and entrepreneurs, driven by the logic of the marketplace and lured by the opportunities of the global economy, are on a lookout for something new and something innovative at all times.

Relative to the rapid pace of economic change, the pace of cultural change is slower because cultural change results from changes in social conventions and institutions which, in turn, result from changes in individual attitudes and values. Nationalism as emotion may actually block cultural change as it tends to resist any change that threatens the traditional ways of doing things which give a group of individuals their common identity. This is one reason why foreign direct investment does not, by itself, translate into economic development for a nation guided by nationalism as emotion. Foreign technologies often require changes in social conventions and institutions in order for them to be effective in bringing about desired economic changes. But social conventions and institutions do not change easily because vested interests work to preserve them while individual attitudes and values are constrained by such feelings as loyalty and patriotism.

If cultural change cannot keep pace with economic change, it is up to the polity to devise ways to maintain the cohesion of the overall social system. While it may be easier for the government guided by nationalism as emotion to maintain that cohesion internally, no government can afford to be guided by nationalism as emotion in an interdependent world. Economic development is best achieved by participating in the world economy, as that will provide a nation opportunities to benefit from economies of scale. If exposure to global market capitalism threatens national identity, it is the job of the polity to cultivate an awareness among the people that there is no national development today unless nationalism as emotion is successfully transcended.

Conclusion

A nation as a unit of social life is an evolutionary product and, as such, cannot claim to be the final and ideal form of organizing social life (Hobsbawn [1990]). As its evolutionary environment undergoes changes at all times, no nation will remain as a stable social system for long regardless of what defines that nation as a unit—land, language, race, or religion.

While many national groups aspire to achieve political autonomy guided by their own versions of nationalism as emotion, no nation today can carve out a path of national development independently of other nations as it is enveloped in a network of global interdependence culturally, economically and politically. This does not deny the role of nationalism as emotion as a source of national pride and a vehicle for promoting solidarity among a group of individuals. The message to be learned by all nations is that, to the extent that global interdependence is a fact of social life, there is no place for nationalism as emotion because it defines the sense of national identity in terms exclusively of one land, one language, one race, or one religion.

The path of national development is full of pitfalls today because the world of global interdependence permits no luxury of waiting for the maturation of domestic social systems. Every nation is entangled in a complicated network of transactions with other nations culturally, economically, and politically. As such, national development for every nation requires careful balancing of the desire for national self-determination on the one hand and the necessity of partaking in the network of global transactions on the other.

The complexity in the patterns of global interdependence today suggests that the nation-state, whether guided by nationalism as ideology or nationalism as emotion, may have outlived its usefulness. Although nationality is regarded as one of the basic human rights as witness the United Nations' *Universal Declaration of Human Rights*, the whole issue of citizenship is becoming less important and less relevant in many areas of social life. Yet no new form of organizing social life has emerged as an effective substitute for the nation-state. Again we seem to be confronted with the problem of maturation, not for this nation or that but for man as a species. Perhaps the current zeal over nationalism is a passing phase in the evolution of our species. However, as Vaclav Havel aptly remarks, "a great deal of time will have to elapse before the emergence of a society that will value national identity but will not raise it above all other values" (Havel [1992], p.15).

PART FOUR

THE WORLD IN TRANSITION

10. CULTURAL DIFFUSION, ECONOMIC INTEGRATION AND THE SOVEREIGNTY OF THE NATION-STATE

Introduction

While the durability of laws and institutions is desirable if they are to ensure a stable environment for social change, existing laws and institutions, as human inventions, are destined to be made inadequate and obsolete by new developments and events in social life. Moreover, when the effects of these developments and events are not confined to the nation where they originate but spread quickly across national borders, threats to existing laws and institutions are more acutely felt by all nations of the world.

No nation of the world is today completely shielded from the effects of social change taking place elsewhere in the world. If the movement of people is still subject to economic and legal constraints, things and news move about across national borders quickly and freely thanks to the phenomenal advances made in this century in transportation and communications technologies. As a result, every nation now finds itself in a difficult, if not hopeless, position of having to defend its sovereignty, constantly pressed to adapt its laws and institutions to the ever-changing realities of an interdependent world. In fact, some recent developments and events in social life have been so disruptive to the sovereignty of the nation-state that the question of whether the continued existence of the nation-state is essential for the maintenance of order in world affairs needs to be subjected to serious reexamination.

Cultural Diffusion

"Cultural diffusion" is one type of social change which every nation has been subject to in recent decades. The phenomenon of cultural diffusion includes diversification of life-styles and dispersion of value systems which modern liberal democratic states have been, in a way, promoting with their guarantee of individual freedom in cultural life. However, what is more serious as a threat to the sovereignty of the nation-state is the presence of minority groups which form nations within a nation in the conduct of their cultural life. With strong allegiance to their ethnic heritage, religious belief or linguistic preference, these minority groups oppose—sometimes with violence—the overall social policy of the nation. Nations as diverse as Belgium, Canada, India, Iraq, Ireland, Spain and Sri Lanka share this problem, hit by occasional outbursts of separatist movements by minority groups who demand autonomy in the running of their affairs. Nations such as England, France and Germany are experiencing a similar problem as migrant workers from Third World nations have now established themselves as minority groups in these host nations. Needless to say, the migration of workers looking for economic opportunities is not limited to these countries.

Cultural diffusion does not require the movement of people with the development of the global communications network. A recent decision (in May 1987) of the U.S. Supreme Court to label as "political propaganda" Canadian documentary films dealing with acid rain and nuclear war offers an intriguing case in that the Court appealed to the Foreign Agents Registration Act passed in 1942 when restricting the movement of people and objects still constituted an effective protection against the infiltration of foreign ideas and values. The arrival of satellite broadcasting has made it impossible for the governments of many East and Central European nations to retain their authority over the cultural life of their citizens. Although the ownership of satellite dishes can be prohibited, these governments cannot prevent their citizens from obtaining, by either manufacturing or importing, television sets that can receive satellite broadcasts originating in their Western neighbors.

The sovereignty of the nation-state has also come to be tested by cultural movements that transcend national boundaries. The rise of Islamic Fundamentalism is a dramatic example of this type of movement. There are, of course, other transnational organizations such as Amnesty International, the International Red Cross and Physicians for Social Responsibility whose ideas can affect the cultural life of many nations, to the extent that they are successful in influencing national governments to revise their laws and institutions.

Economic Integration

"Economic integration" is another type of social change which has come to undermine the sovereignty of the nation-state. To begin with, the dramatic expansion of international trade since the end of World War II which has outpaced the growth in the world's production of goods and services, while no doubt spreading the benefits of trade to many nations, has added another thorny issue of protecting and promoting national interests over which one government fights with other governments. A far more serious threat to national sovereignty comes from the activities of multinational corporations. With their financial assets spread across many international financial markets and their production facilities scattered all over the globe, large multinational corporations today control economic fortunes far exceeding those of most nation-states. Multinational corporations are not subject to policies and regulations of any single nation as they can easily leave one nation and move to another where they can expect a more favorable treatment for their activities from the host government. Some multinational corporations go as far as engaging in covert operations to undermine the host government if they do not find it to their liking.

The integration of economic life has also enhanced the chances of industrial pollution spreading across national borders. Europeans were reminded of their ecological interdependence when, on November 1, 1986, a fire at Sandoz, the Swiss chemical company located in the border city of Basel, spilled toxic waste into the Rhine, killing fish and damaging water quality along the river. This and other cases of industrial pollution, including the case of acid rain contested between England and the Scandinavian nations and between Canada and the United States, illustrates how economic activities and their repercussions can no longer be contained within national borders.

The sovereignty of developing nations has been under challenge for some time now by the private banks of developed nations from whom they have been borrowing large sums of investment funds. One after another of these debtor nations experienced difficulties in meeting their payment obligations in 1980s, culminating, in March 1987, in the announcement by the Brazilian government to suspend interest and principal payments it owed to foreign banks. The Brazilian case points up a truly perplexing aspect of the sovereignty issue, for the Brazilian government justified its unilateral act of renouncing its financial obligations by arguing that its responsibility is to the nation and not to foreign banks.

Challenges which cultural diffusion and economic integration present to the sovereignty of the nation-state are thus both internal and external. That is to say, cultural diffusion and economic integration not only erode the authority of the state over individuals, groups and associations within the nation but also undermine the independence of the state from other nations in the running of its domestic affairs. The upshot is that the nation-state now finds itself to be at the same time too large for maintaining the cohesion of cultural life and too small for coordinating the complexity of economic life.

Culture, Economy and Polity

That the nation-state has become too large for cultural life and too small for economic life is, actually, a necessary consequence of the fundamental conflict among culture, economy and polity as the interdependent yet different spheres of human activity. Culture, economy and polity differ from one another in at least three important ways. First, culture, economy and polity differ in "the hierarchy of needs" that they serve. Culture, defined here as "the set of all human actions pertaining to the creation and dissemination of ideas, symbols and values", serves the spiritual need of the individual human being who seeks meaning behind the scheme of things in the world around him. Economy, or "the set of all human actions pertaining to the production and distribution of goods and services", defines the sphere of human activity which has to do with satisfying the material need of the individual. Finally, polity, or "the set of all human actions pertaining to the establishment and preservation of law and order", is the sphere of human activity founded on the individual's need for protection and justice in the conduct of his social life.

Culture, economy and polity also differ from one another with respect to "the field of action". Cultural life, as it has to do with the spiritual need, is not necessarily tied to a particular geographical area. Although it is true that a certain locality is elevated into a sacred place of worship by adherents of a certain religion, cultural ideas, symbols and values can spread from one locality to another and, therefore, easily transcend national boundaries. Economic life also transcends national boundaries with ease, for the logic of the marketplace does not necessarily honor differences in cultural values or political systems. Political life, in contrast, is always bound to a territory, for "the first duty of the sovereign" is, as Adam Smith put it, "that of protecting the society from the violence and invasion of other independent societies" (Smith [1937], p.653).

Culture, economy and polity further differ from one another with respect to "the manner of influence". While in the cultural arena, cultural groups fight over which ideas, symbols and values will command the following of the people, in the economic arena economic organizations compete over which goods and services will win the patronage of the consuming public. In politics, which parties and policies will win out is decided by the political power of one form or another, which sometimes takes the form of naked force and other times of the number of votes cast in the ballot box (Russell [1938]).

Reflecting as it does these differences in the hierarchy of needs, the field of action and the manner of influence, the fundamental conflict among culture, economy and polity exists at the national as well as the global level. In fact, the growth of modern nation-states owes largely to the widespread acceptance of the idea that this conflict can be resolved at the national level if polity could subjugate culture and economy in the name of national unity. The autonomy of culture and economy was permitted only to the extent that it would not undermine the supremacy of polity in the running of national affairs. Today, however, that resolution of the fundamental conflict is inadequate as cultural diffusion and economic integration have brought all nations into contact with one another at the global level. We are indeed living in a new world now and, therefore, need a new political philosophy which explicitly addresses itself to the new realities of global interdependence.

Resolving the Conflict among Culture, Economy and Polity

Some may argue that the only viable resolution of the fundamental conflict is for each nation to become an autonomous unit in all three spheres of human activity. However, it seems highly unlikely that nations of the world today would revert to this form of organizing their national affairs. Although a "successful" autonomy of the nation-state is not without historical precedent (as was the case with Tokugawa Japan under its isolationist policy), most nations of the world today are too committed, justifiably, to the idea that individual freedom in cultural and economic life is the key to improving both quality of life and standard of living.

Others may argue that the resolution of the fundamental conflict at the global level can be achieved only by working towards the construction of the world-state. Given that the conflict is beyond the control of any single nation-state, this may appear to be the only logical way out. After all, if a social system is to be viable, it is essential that some type of political institution oversee, if not control, cultural and economic activities so that they will not disturb the overall stability of the system. The world-state, they would argue, would be a natural candidate for taking up that function of an overseer for the world as a social system. Perhaps the threat of nuclear annihilation, which has made the concept of "national defense" totally meaningless, may, in a sort of devious way, bring nations of the world together. Should this happen, it would indeed be a great accomplishment for our species. As things stand now, however, it is unlikely that the world-state would become anything more than just another transnational institution, like the current United Nations which merely serves as an arena for resolving conflicts among nation-states, nations and minority groups.

Given that culture, economy and polity represent three aspects of human activity which address themselves to different human needs, any successful resolution of the fundamental conflict among them at the global level must be one which accommodates these different needs for what they are worth. In other words, it is essential that we accept the idea that the world is a system consisting of culture, economy and polity as three integral component subsystems. Culture, economy and polity, as subsystems, can in turn be seen as consisting, respectively, of cultural groups, of economic organizations, and of political institutions.

The Nation-State in the New World of Global Interdependence

What should be the role of the nation-state in our revisionist conception of the world as an eco-system consisting of the full diversity of cultural groups, economic organizations and political institutions? Each nation-state will have to play the role of maintaining law and order in a specific geographical area which, for historical or other reasons, defines a nation. Emphasis here is on "geographical area" (with appropriate consideration being given to the surrounding airspace and waters), for territoriality, or jurisdiction over people and things in a geographical area, should be the central organizing principle of defining an autonomous political unit. The question of whether a minority group should be granted an independent status should also be judged on this principle, i.e., whether granting autonomy to a minority group best contributes to the maintenance of law and order in a specific geographical area.

Making "jurisdiction over people and things in a geographical area" the central organizing principle in polity means that the role of the nation-state should be diminished from the spheres of culture and economy whose "fields of actions" are not constrained by territoriality. The nation-state has appealed, too often in the past, to the idea of national identity in times of international conflict. However, the question of identity has to do with finding self-identity and should be left to individual cultural life. We are already witnessing a whole array of international cultural associations, groups and movements operating on the world stage. These associations, groups and movements will continue to fight among themselves over which ideas, symbols and values will win the hearts and minds of the people. As long as this fight is in the open marketplace of ideas, symbols and values, the situation is far less harmful than when each nation-state employs its political—and sometimes military—muscle to promote a specific cultural system it endorses.

The nation-state has played, and continues to play, an important role in protecting and promoting national interests in the international economic arena. Protective tariffs and quotas are imposed by governments for no other reason than to protect special interest groups at home. Most nation-states are also captives of what might be termed "GNP fetishism" and zealously pursue macroeconomic policies to promote economic growth as measured by the Gross National Product. However, when the world economy has become as interdependent as it is today, there is no justification for nation-states to continue to concern themselves exclusively with "the wealth of nations". The central concern of all nations should be "the wealth of humankind", which requires cooperation and coordination of economic activities at the global level.

Even with these reformulations of the idea of the nation-state, conflicts and disputes among nation-states will not easily disappear as culture, economy and polity interact with one another at the global level today in a complicated web of actions, reactions and repercussions. For such a complicated social system to function, existing laws and institutions which regulate various international and transnational activities will have to be reformed. This includes a fundamental reform of the United Nations to become a "head", rather than a "center", of world affairs so that a resolution agreed on there would carry binding power over member nations in such areas as the violation of basic human rights and covert operations by one nation-state to undermine the stability of other nation states. In the economic arena it would be necessary, sooner or later, to reorganize the World Bank as the central bank of the world economy with the power to issue money and coordinate macroeconomic policies for the common interests of humankind.

Conclusion

Needless to say, no reform in laws and institutions is sufficient unless it is accompanied by a change in people's consciousness. Just as the modern nation-state has grown out of a consciousness reformation regarding our conception of the rights of the individual and the state, any new world system, if it is to evolve as a viable system, must be the result of a consciousness reformation about our conception of man as an individual and as a species.

The world faces a crisis today because nation-states, which have outlived their usefulness in maintaining world order, still struggle to reassert their lost sovereignty over human affairs. The crisis will not go away as long as nation-states are guided solely by their concern over their own national interests in world affairs.

What is missing in the world today is the unity of vision and purpose which is needed to define what constitutes the common interests of humankind and the basic rights of individuals. Without vision an international law would at best be a temporary expediency and without purpose an international treaty would lack the binding power of a moral imperative. If we are to establish any semblance of order in world affairs, it is vital that we work towards developing the unity of vision and purpose. And the unity of vision and purpose must ultimately be sought in the realm of the human mind. For, as Thomas Jefferson clearly realized, "laws and institutions must go hand in hand with the progress of the human mind" (Pedover [1939], p.32).

11. GLOBAL INTERDEPENDENCE AND THE PATTERNS OF INTERACTION AND TRANSFORMATION OF HUMAN SYSTEMS

Introduction

Globalization is a driving force which permeates all spheres of human activity in the world today. But nowhere is the push towards globalization as evident and strong as it is in the economic arena. Economics emerged as an important agent of social change when the Industrial Revolution ushered in the age of symbiotic relationship between business and technology. And the scope of influence that economics exerts on human affairs has steadily expanded since the nineteenth century when the idea of commerce as an agent for social progress was vigorously promoted by the Philosophical Radicals.

If the globalization of the economy is not a new phenomenon, there are new developments and events in the world economy which are transforming the old conception of the world as a system consisting of autonomous nation-states. These new developments and events suggest the emergence of a new type of global interdependence whose impact goes beyond the economic arena. The purpose of this chapter is to examine what kinds of interaction and transformation are taking place among the world's diverse human systems, not only among business firms and economic organizations but also among families, schools, governments and other supporting human systems as these human systems are increasingly brought into the network of global interdependence.

New Realities of Global Economic Interdependence

How international trade has steadily expanded since the end of World War II as measured, for example, by the ratio of exports over the gross national product is a familiar story by now. However, as the scope as well as the volume of trade have expanded, the conventional definition of international trade as trade "between" nations has come to be increasingly questioned for its relevance. In fact, the label "Made in ..." no longer does justice to the realities of world trade unless we examine in detail who is doing the making and where.

The erosion of the meaning of "international trade" owes a great deal to the expansion of activities by multinational corporations. Multinational corporations can easily shift the main focus of their activities from trade to direct investment, as they do to get around the protective measures taken by national governments. Many multinational corporations are now engaged in so-called "reverse imports" as their overseas operations become more cost-efficient than their home operations, or in "revolving exports" by first exporting technology to one nation to set up production operations and then exporting products produced there to other nations.

Foreign direct investment by multinational corporations is not a new phenomenon; it has historically played an important role in transferring technologies from developed to developing countries. What is new is the swiftness with which multinational corporations shift their operations from one country to another to take advantage of differences in labor costs, exchange rates and political environments. Since creating and maintaining jobs is an important concern of politicians everywhere, governments, especially at the local level, are forced into a feverish race to make their communities attractive to foreign direct investment by multinational corporations. Not only do they try to rebuild their old infrastructure but they also engage in public relations activities to advertise the receptiveness of their communities to guests from abroad.

While local governments—and local residents—are busy making adjustments in their communities, national governments are busy making adjustments in domestic laws and institutions to the new realities of global economic interdependence. These adjustments include modifications in safety standards in the workplace, adoption of tighter emission controls in factories, rewriting of tax codes, and even changes in people's value systems. National governments are also involved in the task of working out the differences among their domestic economic policies—in the enforcement of anti-monopoly laws, for example. Further, in an effort to mitigate the impact of external shocks and disturbances on their domestic economies, policy-makers have started to coordinate their macroeconomic policies as is typified by the annual "summit" of the leaders of the Group of Seven nations.

Challenges to Conventional Wisdom

These new developments and events in the world economy challenge our conventional wisdom about the meaning of international trade, the role of government in the economy, the notion of social responsibility of business, and other issues related to economic activities. For one thing, it is clear that the nation-state is no longer the only relevant unit in thinking about international trade. While national governments have traditionally been concerned with the question of protecting and promoting their own national interests, many governments are beginning to realize that conflicts among national interests and differences in policies among nations need to be coordinated in the interest of the general welfare, which the conventional wisdom of policy-makers today dictates that the world economy be kept viable and stable.

While domestic laws and institutions can no doubt be changed to meet the demands of global economic interdependence, some changes are easier to make than others. It is also to be noted that the swiftness with which these changes are made differs from one country to another, reflecting the differences in the effectiveness of the government as a "decider", as James Miller puts it, in society seen as a living system (Miller [1978]). The degree to which the government is involved in the management of the economy also differs significantly from one country to another. As a matter of fact, the success of East Asian countries in the Pacific Rim region in international trade in the last few decades has revived interest in the paternalistic role the government plays in these countries with the Confucian cultural tradition (Tai [1989]).

The phenomenon of global economic interdependence is especially pronounced in the realm of financial transactions. Thanks to advances made in information and communications technologies, a single world-wide financial market has emerged, resulting in a phenomenal increase in the amount of currencies, bonds and stocks transacted across national boundaries.

The emergence of the global financial market and the expanded scope of "transnational" activities by multinational corporations seriously undermine the government's ability to manage the economy. All governments—large and small, liberal and conservative—must pay close attention to what is happening in the global economy if they are to be effective in maintaining the stability of their economies. The conduct of domestic economic policies without taking into account the effects of external shocks and disturbances on the conduct of the domestic economy or, for that matter, the effects of domestic policies on the conduct of the global economy will carry a severe penalty in the form of imported inflation or unemployment, or a change in the amount of capital outflow or inflow.

One important consequence of global economic interdependence is that economic policy-making today is less subject to the whims of policy-makers as all governments are forced to play by the rules of the global marketplace. This does not mean, however, that the world economy has been transformed into a stable system. It means that the world economy will instead be subject to the whims of the marketplace, with the possibility of a traumatic episode taking place from time to time as witness the Great Crash of 1987.

Etherealization and Materialization

The new realities of global interdependence in the economic arena are forcing all nations of the world to make changes, to a greater or lesser extent, in their human systems—and the laws and regulations which affect the operation of these human systems. The changes in human systems which are taking place around us today can be classified into two types of "bottom-up" and "top-down" changes. "Bottom-up" changes reflect what might be termed the process of "etherealization" in the evolution of social systems, while "top-down" changes reflect the process of "materialization".

"Bottom-up" changes in human systems, which reflect the process of "etherealization", refer to changes in human systems which are made in response to new developments and events in the economy. These are called bottom-up changes because the economy forms the "infrastructure", as opposed to the "superstructure", in the Marxian conception of a social system consisting of economy and culture. Maslow's conception of the hierarchy of human needs also supports our characterization of this type of change as a bottom-up variety, for changes in the economy, which serves the lower needs of material existence, are forcing changes in political and other social institutions, which serve the higher needs of man as a social being (Maslow [1970]). In short, a social system transforms itself from below, or "etherealizes" itself, as a result of changes coming from the infrastructure of the economy.

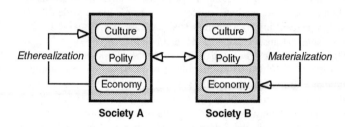

In contrast, a social system transforms itself from above, or "materializes" itself, when changes in people's ideas and values trigger changes in laws and regulations which affect the operation of human systems. This type of transformation is termed the process of "materialization" in the sense that changes in abstract ideas and values filter down to changes in human systems which foster social life. These changes are called "top-down" changes because the impetus for changes comes from culture, or the "superstructure" of a social system.

Examples of bottom-up changes include the deregulation of domestic markets (in the telecommunications industry, for example) in response to competitive pressure in the global marketplace, the adoption of a new standard in working hours, the modification of domestic safety standards in the workplace to reflect international standards, and educational reform to enhance the competitiveness of the domestic economy. Many other changes of bottom-up varieties are in the offing in such areas as patent laws, intellectual property rights, measurement systems, and even the question of which side of the road cars and trucks ought to be driven.

On the other hand, human systems experience top-down changes as a result of the influx of new ideas and values from abroad. Top-down changes may also come about as a result of the emergence of influential leaders in cultural life. On a smaller scale, this type of change takes place all the time at the level of a corporation, an organization, a local community, or a nation-state. In the case of the emergence of a truly influential leader in religion or other cultural systems, top-down changes can easily cross national borders and induce transformation of human systems in other societies.

It was Schumpeter who drew our attention to the strategic importance of what he termed "creative destruction" as an essential feature of economic development under capitalism (Schumpeter [1949]). However, creative destruction on the global scale will be self-defeating, for unconstrained and uncoordinated economic activities will surely bring about what Hardin called "the tragedy of the commons" sooner or later (Hardin [1968]). As people have become increasingly aware of the impact of economic activities on the global environment, the recycling of resources and reduction in wastes are being incorporated into an integral part of economic life, from business organizations to civic groups to school education. This is another example of a top-down change we observe in the world around us.

To the extent that the globalization of economic activities for the past century or so has sprouted from the idea of the Philosophical Radicals, what appear to be bottom-up changes may well be instances of top-down changes in human systems. In other words, ideas and events do tend to interact in the cybernetic process called human history. This interpretation is consistent with the Toynbeean view of history as the continual process of challenges and responses among cultural systems (Toynbee [1954]). If we tend to get the impression that most changes taking place in the world today are of the bottom-up variety, it is because changes in the economy are much faster than changes in other social subsystems.

Conclusion

Whether changes taking place around us in human systems are of the bottom-up or top-down variety, i.e., whether the transformations the world's social systems are going through today are mostly of etherealization-type or of materialization-type, there is no question that economics has become a powerful agent of social change in the modern world. This means that other aspects of social life also need to be reformed if the world enveloped in the network of global interdependence is to function as a viable and stable system.

Globalization, by definition, means that more and more people become involved in the making of a new world as a social system. This means, therefore, that the world is going to witness more incidents of economic friction and cultural confrontation than we have seen in the past unless people are guided in their activities by their "top-down" awareness about the realities of global interdependence. Every social system is thus confronted with the challenge of adapting itself to the realities of global interdependence as it strives to reform its human systems—from families to schools, and from communities to workplaces.

12. HISTORY AS A SYSTEMS SCIENCE

Introduction

Dr. Johnson defines history as "a narration of events and facts delivered with dignity" in his *The Dictionary of the English Language*. Reading great historians, like Herodotus, Thucydides and Tacitus, certainly confirms the aptness of this definition, for their narratives not only succeed in vividly recreating historical events for us but are delivered with such authority that we are invariably left with a few lessons about the foibles of individual actors and the vicissitudes of societal fortunes. Great historians manage to deliver lessons of history with dignity because they practice their trade with care and deliberation, fully realizing what a delicate and difficult task they face as they try to balance between fact and hearsay, between observation and speculation.

History as a discipline, because it requires a delicate and difficult balancing between fact and hearsay, between observation and speculation, is difficult to characterize as strictly a humanities discipline. Rather, it is destined to oscillate between sciences and humanities. It is not surprising, then, if historians have allied themselves with a whole array of different approaches, ranging from quantitative analysis to romantic storytelling to psycho-analysis.

While each approach has its own merits and offers valuable insight into an aspect of human affairs, historians have thus far failed to develop a unified methodology which treats the historical process as a process of interaction among individual actors, groups and organizations operating in diverse social systems in the world characterized by the phenomena of global interdependence. What we propose to do in this chapter is to expand our analysis of the world of global interdependence to include a study of history and suggest a minimal set of basic premises which need to be incorporated in developing the methodology of history as a systems science, thus extending and adapting the methodology of general system theory to the analysis and interpretation of the historical process. A systems approach to history should facilitate our endeavor to derive lessons of history more relevant to our interdependent world, for systems scientists who deal with human affairs do so with explicit recognition of the need to examine the ways in which individuals and societies interact with one another as open systems. If our past behavior has pointed up our propensity not to learn lessons from history, we would certainly like our history to tell us why this has been the case.

Approaches to History

History as a discipline, i.e., as a systematic endeavor to learn truths about the historical process, involves two basic acts on the part of the historian as the practitioner of this discipline. On the one hand, it involves the act of "knowing" about the historical data to be gathered and reported. On the other, it involves the act of "narrating" the historical process based on analysis and interpretation of the historical data.

The data set from which historians develop their narratives consists of events, peoples, phenomena, and things. Events like wars and revolutions have always attracted the attention of historians. In fact, some historians consider their role to be that of the narrator of events; to these historians, history is basically the history of events, or *l'histoire événementielle*. On the other hand, there is a large group of historians who subscribe to what Boulding calls the "Great Men" theory of history (Boulding [1978]). According to these historians, like Thomas Carlyle, history is very much a matter of telling stories about heroic figures accomplishing heroic deeds which bring about dramatic changes in their societies and the world. Historians have also looked into various natural and social phenomena such as diseases, social conventions and institutions. Thus books have been written on the history of "yellow fever", "diplomacy", and "the prison system". History can further be told in terms of "things"—materials and technologies—which humans have exploited in the conduct of their affairs (Heilbroner [1967]). Thus, an early history of our species is often characterized as going through the Stone Age, the Bronze Age, and the Iron Age.

The development of modern human sciences has contributed to the multiplicity of approaches to history as these sciences have provided valuable tools for analyzing and interpreting the historical data. Such disciplines as anthropology, economics, psychology, and sociology have greatly contributed to the richness and scope of the historian's analysis and interpretation of the historical data.

That scientific methods are employed in the analysis and interpretation of the historical data does not by itself guarantee that the narratives of scientific historians are more objective and reliable than those of humanistically oriented historians. As a matter of fact, a scientific method can be employed to confirm—even promote—a specific paradigm in a scientific discipline. This is the danger that Habermas cautions us when he talks about the use of "retrospective econometrics" to confirm the neoclassical paradigm in economics (Habermas [1979]). Indeed, what insight do we gain from an analysis of the behavior of hunter-gatherers 10,000 years ago based on the rational choice model of "economic man"? The same can be said of a psychoanalytic study of the motivations behind heroic deeds of great men in history. Martin Luther may well have been acting out his rebellion against his domineering father when he challenged the authority of the Church of Rome (Erikson [1958]). But the fact of the matter is that an event like the Reformation is a "systemic" event involving the interplay of many factors—political, cultural, economic, as well as psychological.

History as a Systems Science

There are several compelling reasons why history needs to be treated as a systems science. In the first place, the relationship between the historian and the historical data is exactly the kind of relationship we find between the systems scientists and the systems that they study. The historian as the researcher must rely on some "theory" in order to decide what kind of data need to be gathered and reported, and the historian as the narrator must choose some perspective from which to describe these data.

Second, history, like systems sciences, deals with events, peoples, phenomena, and things which are not subject to the law of "linear causality" which is found in classical sciences. Although the historian may be tempted, as such an eminent historian as E.H. Carr himself admits [1964], to apply the logic of linear causality to the historical process and describe how one thing "inevitably" leads to another, something like the law of "equifinality" found in systems sciences is at work behind the historical process (Bertalanffy [1968]). Or, as Tolstoy aptly put it, "[h]istory appears to us as a certain combination of freedom and inevitability." Because both freedom and inevitability are involved, the historical process is full of surprises as every human action is bound to have "unintended consequences".

Third, the historical process, i.e., the evolution of human societies which historians concern themselves with, takes place in the space of interaction among social systems, with each social system constituting an open system with respect to other societies and the natural environment. In other words, the proper study of history is the behavior of open systems. To be sure, some historians concern themselves with the history of a specific society, of a specific land, of a specific nation. But unless such an idiographic study is combined with the nomothetic study of societies treated as open systems, they will not be able to derive meaningful "lessons of history" which can be used as universal guides for behavior. And most historians are aware that their kind of studies will be duplicated by other historians studying about other societies.

Fourth, history is a fertile ground for applications of general system theory in that it requires applications of insights developed in many diverse scientific disciplines in analyzing and interpreting the historical data. In addition to human sciences such as anthropology, economics, psychology, and sociology, natural sciences such as biology, chemistry, geology, and physics can play useful roles here as they have done so already in many works.

There are some historians who have employed, wittingly or unwittingly, what we are characterizing here as "a systems approach" to history. Although their claim to the "historical truth" of their analyses may have been somewhat discounted by the dramatic events that took place in Eastern Europe in the last few years, Marx and Engels can still be regarded as the early practitioners of a systems approach when they proclaimed, in their *Manifesto of the Communist Party,* that "[t]he history of all hitherto existing society is the history of class struggles."

They are credited with the application of the dialectic method of Hegel which involves the interplay of two counteracting forces in the historical process.

Max Weber's analysis of the role of the Protestant ethic in the rise of capitalism is another example of a systems approach to history in that he was concerned with the problem of how the psychological attitude of a group of individuals operating within a specific cultural system might influence their behavior in business enterprises (Weber [1930]). The role of "attitudes" is also emphasized by the Annals school of historians such as Lucien Febre in his conception of *l'histoire psychologique* and Fernand Braudel in his search for *la longue durée* and *mentalité* (Braudel [1981]). Spengler went a step further than these historians in that it was he who suggested how a certain attitude, like the propensity to seek transcendence, might be influenced by characteristics of the natural environment surrounding certain societies (Spengler [1928]).

When we speak of practitioners of a systems approach to history, we cannot neglect the work of Toynbee (Toynbee [1954]). Toynbee's view of history as the process of challenges and responses of civilizations is important because he treats history as the process of eco-systemic interaction among "open" social systems. The historical dimension comes into play because each social system, representing as it does a specific civilization, embodies in its behavior its own institutional memories. In a recent work, Kennedy investigates one aspect of such challenges and responses in the form of military conflict (Kennedy [1987]). Kennedy applies a Parsonian view of societal evolution in drawing his lessons about the economic fortunes of nations as they try to maintain and promote their military strength (Parsons [1967]).

Two Lessons of History

History is to be treated as a systems science because the historical process is a process which takes place in the space of eco-systemic interaction among social systems, with each social system consisting of individual actors who operate themselves in the space spanned by their cultural, economic and political actions. Individual actors and social systems embody certain characteristics, which we formulate as the basic postulates of history as a systems science.

The first postulate has to do with the role of an individual actor in the historical process and may be termed the postulate of "multiple potentialities":

Postulate I (**Multiple Potentialities**): An individual actor in the historical process embodies and, hence, has the potential of projecting in his behavior all the accumulated characteristics of his society and his species.

Every individual, whether he realizes or not, is a historical being in the sense that he is at the same time a biological being, a social being, and a cultural being. As such, he inherits what his society and his species have accomplished, adds something to that heritage, and passes on the collected accomplishments of his society and his species to later generations. As Shakespeare puts it, "[t]here is a history in all men's lives." This postulate thus expresses, in most general terms, the basic premise of general system theory that an individual human being is an open system. Every action of an individual actor is full of potentialities because what his action does and means to him and to his society depends on the manner of interaction with other individual actors in his and other societies.

The second postulate about the historical process addresses itself to the manner of interaction among individual actors and societies. It will be referred to as the postulate of "complex interdependence":

> *Postulate II* (**Complex Interdependence**): An individual actor operates within a social system which is entangled in a network of complex interdependence with other social systems in all aspects of his social life— culturally, economically, and politically.

The postulate of complex interdependence states that there are multiple channels of linkages and connections among social systems because the social life of an individual entails interactions with other individuals in his and other societies culturally, economically as well as politically (Keohane and Nye [1977]).

When one individual purchases a commodity at a store, for example, he is already engaged in a complex pattern of interaction with other individuals, other societies, and the natural environment. This is so because the production of a commodity is organized by a corporation registered in a certain society, operating in a certain cultural environment, employing natural as well as human resources, following the rules and regulations established by one government (or many governments in the case of a multinational corporation), and exploiting a technology which has been developed by generations of scientists and engineers.

The postulates of multiple potentialities and complex interdependence are the two threads of history which connect all individuals vertically through time with their past and their future as well as horizontally across space with other individuals in other societies. These two postulates together imply that the historical process is not subject to the law of linear causality. Instead, we have:

> *The Law of Mutual Causal Dependence:* Actions in the historical process are subject to the law of mutual causal dependence in which one action is at the same time the cause and effect of other actions.

The fact that all actions in the historical process are subject to the law of mutual causal dependence is not, by itself, something to be deplored. While mutual causal dependence may lead to catastrophe in some cases, it also suggests possibilities for synergistic cooperations among individual actors and social organizations. What is to be deplored is the fact that mutual causal dependence too often results in conflicts and frictions. Why, then, is the historical process full of conflicts and frictions? This is an outcome of two additional postulates about the perceptive capacity of individual actors and the nature of their social interaction.

> *Postulate III* (**Faulty Perception**): An individual actor in the historical process is guided in his behavior by subjective models of reality which,

because of the faulty nature of human perception, fail to capture the full extent of multiple potentialities and complex interdependence.

Human actions, even spontaneous ones, stem from some models of reality. These models of reality formed in the space of perception do not capture realities *in toto*. This means that even contemplated actions can at best accomplish what Simon calls "bounded rationality" (Simon [1982]). In one way or another, human perception is defective as it fails to perceive the full extent of the consequences of actions, reactions and repercussions.

In addition to the faulty nature of human perception, there is a matter of systemic incongruence for any social system.

***Postulate IV* (Systemic Dissonance):** A social system is inflicted with systemic dissonance because culture, economy and polity as subsystems operate on mutually incongruent principles.

Culture, economy and polity, as subsystems of a social system, are subject to different laws of operation as they address themselves to different needs and aspirations of individuals as cultural beings, economic beings and political beings. To the extent that social systems are inflicted with systemic dissonance, the historical process as a process of eco-systemic interaction among social systems is subject to what might be called the law of "inherent instability":

The *Law of Inherent Instability*: Conflicts and frictions among individuals, groups, organizations and social systems are inherent features of the historical process.

As social animals, we humans need our societies to make us human. However, forming societies requires that conflicts between individual interests and the overall interest of societies to preserve social order, for example, must somehow be resolved. The fact that we are all concerned about protecting our own individual interests means that we bring our "unsociable sociality", as Kant put it, to forming our social systems. And this unsociable sociality in all of us, which is expressed sometimes against other individuals and sometimes against other groups of individuals from different ethnic origins, religious orientations or nationalities, is at the root of conflicts and frictions in our social life. It is not necessary to look far into the past to see how our history is a history of conflicts and frictions. What many societies are going through today amply illustrates the law of inherent instability.

Man as a cultural being seeks his identity by associating himself with an ethnic group, a language, or a religion. This cultural need comes into conflict with the economic need or desire to raise the standard of living which is satisfied by creating a world-wide market, crossing cultural boundaries. If incongruence between cultural and economic needs leads to conflicts and frictions, polity is the subsystem that tries to resolve and mediate these conflicts and frictions. However, the political need for maintaining sovereignty and autonomy of a region, or a group of individuals, again comes into conflict with cultural and economic needs.

The inherent instability of our social systems has global implications now because the nation-state, as a product of nineteenth-century historical consciousness, cannot be depended on as facilitator of conflicts and frictions among diverse social groups operating in today's interdependent world. In fact, systemic dissonance among culture, economy and polity is now an inherent feature of the world as a system because of the phenomena of global interdependence. Consider, for example, the case of some nations imposing economic sanctions against other nations claimed to be violating basic human rights. This political measure obviously runs counter to the economic interests of protecting domestic producers and creating jobs in the domestic market.

Conclusion

The law of mutual causal dependence is a restatement of the basic proposition in general system theory that "everything depends on everything else." We are limited in our capacity to perceive correctly and fully the extent of such mutual causal dependence, as is formulated in our postulate of "faulty perception". This is indeed the reason why we humans are destined, in the ultimate sense, never to learn the lessons of history. In other words, the only viable lesson of history is the lesson that we never learn the lessons of history. Or, as Hegel put it, "[w]hat experience and history teach us is that peoples and governments never have learned from history, or acted on principles deduced from it."

This message about our incapacity, along with the law of inherent instability, is enough to drive some people to cynicism. We can certainly sympathize with James Joyce when he lets one of his characters utter: "History is a nightmare from which I am trying to awake." And with the development of modern technologies, we have all become, albeit vicariously, participants and eyewitnesses of the historical process in our interdependent world. Does this mean that history has become a nightmare for all of us?

History as a systems science does point to a way of liberating ourselves from our bondage to the historical process. Although our perceptibility may be limited and although our social life is inflicted with conflicts and frictions, we are adaptive creatures capable of making changes in our ways of conducting our affairs. And historians as systems scientists can certainly expand our perceptibility and sensitivity to the sordid and painful realities of human existence with their judicious analysis and interpretation of the nature of mutual causal dependence and inherent instability.

PART FIVE

COORDINATION AND
HARMONIZATION

---

13. GLOBAL INTERDEPENDENCE AND THE ECOLOGY OF SOCIAL ETHICS

Introduction

When a statement comes from a mystic with rare vision such as William Blake, we naturally tend to treat it as containing profound truth which transcends time and space. But when he stated, "Do what you will, this life's a fiction and is made up of contradiction," Blake may well have anticipated the arrival of the modern age of existential anxiety and value confusion. Despite its original promise, science has, in some ways, added to modern existential anxiety and value confusion. It has certainly failed to replace philosophy and religion as the source of universal values.

The absence of universally acceptable authority in philosophy, religion or science means the absence of a set of ethical principles which has a binding power over people living in different societies of the world. The absence of universally acceptable ethics is rather unfortunate, for it is at the root of many of the conflicts and confrontations among nation-states and ethnic groups that are being reported daily in the world today. Ethnic rivalries, trade frictions, and terrorist attacks are just a few examples of these conflicts and confrontations which threaten the coherence of the world as a system.

Now that all societies of the world are enveloped in the network of global interdependence, any attempt to seek solutions to these conflicts and confrontations that will have a binding power over all the parties involved must include development of a universally acceptable norm of good behavior, or "global ethics". It may be fruitful, in this connection, to examine if social cybernetics can be of value in deriving global ethics. Social cybernetics, since it treats society as a purposeful, self-regulating system, is less subject to the methodological trap called the fact-value dichotomy than other human sciences. It is particularly suited to an examination of the basic question in social ethics: How should society be organized and what norm of good behavior should individuals and groups follow?

The Ecology of Social Ethics

The absence of universally acceptable authority in philosophy, religion or science means that the derivation of global ethics must be based on what might be termed "the ecology of social ethics". Deriving global ethics from "social" ethics rather than from "normative" ethics is preferable because none of these human endeavors has been successful in generating a universally acceptable set of ethical principles.

Religion has played and still plays an important role in many societies as the source of values and ethical principles. Although, as William Blake points out, all religions of the world may be one, the ways in which religion is practiced by ordinary people have not succeeded in generating an ethical code which commands universal acceptance. The emergence of Islamic Fundamentalism, the opposition to birth control by the Church of Rome, and the violent clashes between Protestants and Catholics in Ireland are but a few examples which remind us of the difficulty of relying on religion as the universal guide for behavior.

Science has failed to replace religion as the source of normative ethics because the basic presumption that science is value-free has turned out to be untenable. Although science seeks facts as opposed to values, what constitutes facts needs to be determined by scientists. In other words, facts need to be chosen and, as long as choice is involved, the strict dichotomy between facts and values breaks down. This does not deny that science can be a valuable guide for behavior, providing as it does useful knowledge of the world around us. But science cannot tell us which behavior is good and which bad.

If normative ethics is not the way to go about it, we must turn to social ethics as the foundation for global ethics. And for the world characterized by global interdependence, the derivation of global ethics must be based on the ecology of social ethics. The ecology of social ethics can be developed in three stages. First, we must examine the process by which certain customs and conventions evolve into ethical principles for a given society. Then, these ethical principles derived for one society must be compared and contrasted with those derived for other societies for the existence of common principles. Finally, this type of comparative study of social ethics must be complemented by an examination of the patterns of interaction and transformation of different ethical systems in the context of ecosystemic interaction of societies in the world of global interdependence.

Customs and Conventions

Customs and conventions are usually regarded as forming the origin of social ethics because they constrain individual behavior for the sake of social order. The fundamental dilemma of social ethics is that customs and conventions are "relative" in the sense that they change from time to time and differ from place to place. In fact, customs and conventions in one society can be quite offensive to another society. Yet members of another society cannot neglect these customs and conventions in the world of global interdependence.

The relativity of customs and conventions is behind many of the disputes among nation-states in the area of international trade. While most nations today are ready to subscribe to the principle of free trade, not all nations share the same ideas as to how best to manage the domestic economy. Moreover, the government in every nation is already faced with the difficult task of coordinating among conflicting interests in the domestic economy. This is the reason why what constitutes the fair rules of the game in international trade is given different interpretations by different governments.

A modern nation-state faces a certain dilemma in developing social ethics as long as it is committed to the separation of church and state. The separation of church and state means that ethical principles which individuals derive from religion can conflict with those which the state imposes to regulate the behavior of individuals as societal members. The problem becomes complicated when a religion, as it often does, transcends national boundaries. This is one way in which eco-systemic interactions among social systems come about. While this type of interaction promotes solidarity among the adherents of a faith, it creates an unsettling situation as far as the political question of the sovereignty of a nation-state is concerned. This is one area where modern political philosophy has failed to resolve the fundamental conflict between culture and polity as social subsystems. For, while culture as a type of human activity is not, in general, bounded by geography, polity is territory-bound as it has to do with the sovereignty of a geographical area and the people living in it.

Insights from Social Cybernetics

If philosophy, religion and science all fail to develop global ethics, where should we look for guidance in this matter? Social cybernetics promises to be of value in developing social ethics in that it treats society as a purposeful, self-regulating system. Every society needs a "constitution", or a code of behavior, which will ensure the viability of that society as a system. Each society has its own goals and objectives and sets down acceptable norms of conduct for both individuals and organizations in it. These acceptable norms of conduct, to the extent that they are observed and become part of customs and conventions, evolve into social ethics.

To the extent that society requires steering for its viability, it has to address itself to the basic question of how to reconcile individual freedom with social control. In cases where individual freedom and social control come into conflict, we need to appeal to the hierarchy of ethical principles. There are ultimately two realities concerning human existence in this world. These are man as an individual and man as a species. Which reality takes precedence needs to be settled by something like the idea of logical typing which will lead to a hierarchy among ethical principles. For example, in problems dealing with the environment, the interest of man as a species must take precedence of the private interest of man as an individual if we are to avoid the tragedy of the commons (Hardin [1968]).

Needless to say, no problem can ever be clearly defined as containing purely the species interest or the private interest. As society consists of all kinds of groups and organizations, most social problems involve conflicts of interest among different subsystems operating in different spheres of a social system. Conflicts of interest are unavoidable because culture, economy and polity, as social subsystems, do not address themselves to the same human needs. Nor do they operate on the same set of principles with the same set of goals and objectives. To the extent that these conflicts are among groups and organizations of a single political entity such as a nation-state, they can be reconciled and coordinated in the context of the viability of that overall social system.

There is no reason why conflicts and confrontations among groups and organizations should be limited to those among domestic groups and organizations. Polity can, of course, try to shield domestic culture and economy from influences coming from foreign societies. The Great Wall built by the Qin Dynasty (221-206 B.C.) is symbolic of such an attempt. But it remains only symbolic because, while it may have kept out the barbarians, the society itself was slowly disintegrating with the suppression of its own people. Blessed with the natural borders accorded to an island nation, Japan tried its isolationist policy during the Tokugawa period, with minimal contact with the outside world. While the policy was effective, Japan was able to develop a rather unique culture and a prosperous economy. But the policy could not maintain social order in the face of the rise of the new powerful merchant class and the expansionist policies of the West in the latter half of the nineteenth century.

Eco-systemic Interaction of Social Systems

Social systems come into contact with one another culturally, economically and politically. And as different social systems come into contact with one another, conflicts and frictions among them are unavoidable as different social systems have different ethical systems, reflecting the differences in the customs and conventions which have guided the evolution of these social systems. Even differences in language can lead to conflicts and confrontations as the basic role of language as a communicative and integrative device breaks down.

As more and more nations are brought into the network of economic interdependence, conflicts of national interests and value systems are expected to increase, forcing, in some cases, changes in social institutions and values. Changes in social institutions and values are already taking place, to the extent that nations have become aware of the realities of global interdependence in the economic arena. Thus, the Japanese now appear ready to abandon the traditional value of sacrificing present consumption for capital accumulation because of the demands made by its trading partners to open up its markets for their products. There are also signs that nations are beginning to realize the importance of coordinating their policies in order to avoid the situation commonly known as the prisoner's dilemma. A protectionist trade policy by one nation, while it promotes special interests of certain groups and organizations within the domestic economy, would be disastrous for the world economy if it invites similar protectionist policies by other nations.

While some institutional changes are easier to make, social institutions tend to resist external pressures for change because they have slowly evolved out of a shared set of values by societal members. The family as a social institution has a long history and is still regarded as the most sacred institution in many societies. The code of good behavior based on a system of reciprocal relationships which maintains the coherence of a family thus plays an important role in regulating individual behavior in these societies. When these societies come into contact with other societies which value individual autonomy in the context of, say, international trade, the former may try to preserve their cultural tradition by restricting trade with the latter.

Even in the absence of direct contact through economic transactions, social systems come into contact with one another with the development of communications technologies. While literacy limits the scope of influence of newspapers, the television, as it appeals to visual perception, has an enormous impact on a much wider audience (Inkels [1988]). Some societies try to disseminate information about other societies using direct broadcasting by satellites. But there are other societies which try to stem the infiltration of cultural values from other societies.

There are some hopeful signs that nations are beginning to realize the importance of behaving responsibly towards the environment. This is one area where the universal norm of good behavior can be developed from a truly species perspective. Moreover, when it comes to man's relation to the natural environment, most religions, with the exception of the historical experience under the Judeo-Christian tradition which the historian White analyzed, agree on the importance of preserving our common heritage (White [1967]). And in this there is no conflict between religious insight and scientific findings about the nature of our ecological interdependence.

Conclusion

While there is little doubt that the world has become an interdependent system, the world as a system is a rather fragile entity whose coherence is constantly threatened by conflicts of interest among individuals, groups, organizations and nations. Since the world lacks an effective decider, conflicts of interest are resolved by compromises and, in some cases, by confrontations. If the world is to function as a viable system, it would be necessary, sooner or later, to develop an effective decider, a world government.

If anything resembling a world government is to emerge, peoples living in different societies need to develop a common purpose and a shared set of values. This is where the real difficulties lie, however. If the oracle does not command universal acceptance, if the prophet or the preacher does not speak for the whole human species, and if the great scientist's insight is bounded by his own cultural heritage, where would one seek the source of a universal value system?

The ecology of social ethics is eminently a pragmatic approach to the search for global ethics, or the universal code of good behavior. However, global ethics would not become global unless it commands respect and obedience by all individuals. Since there are only two realities for man, it is evident that the derivation of global ethics must ultimately rely on our analyses of what principles of good behavior represent the interests of man as a species. But at the moment, no individual, organization or nation seems to speak for the species. Instead, chaos and confusion of values seem to rule world affairs today. As Thomas Huxley pointed out a century ago, we are a unique species in that we have developed the capacity to alter the environment we live in (Huxley [1893]). As a species which has developed the capacity to influence evolution, we owe it to ourselves to try to manage evolution for the benefit of the species. Indeed, deriving global ethics is a question of whether we are responsible for our own fate as a species.

14. EXILES, MIGRANTS AND REFUGEES:
The Nature and Implications of the Movement of People in the World of Global Interdependence

Introduction

Whether biologically so constituted, economically motivated, or politically driven, we humans have always exhibited our propensity to move about from one place to another throughout history. Indeed, the idea of living in a fixed space which agriculture has implanted in our minds appears to be a brief interlude in the history of humans as nomads, with the Industrial Revolution reviving the nomadic propensity of humans in the form of massive movements from rural to urban areas and from developing to developed countries. The globalization of many human activities, from business to science to arts to sports, has dramatically expanded the scope as well as the number of transnational migrants in recent years, prompting one observer to use the term "new Helots" (Cohen [1987]).

While transnational migration is full of personal stories of triumph and tragedy for the individuals involved, it is also a serious social issue in that it imposes social costs not only on the receiving countries but also on the sending countries. And any social problem is, by definition, a global problem in today's world characterized by the ever-expanding network of global interdependence. The purpose of this chapter is, therefore, to examine the nature and implications of the movement of people across national borders in the world of global interdependence.

Why Do People Move Across National Borders?

No individual exercises his free will when he is born into this world as far as choosing his citizenship is concerned. While most individuals lead their lives without having to confront themselves with the issue of making conscious decisions to leave the countries of their birth and to migrate to other countries, it is a fact of life that many individuals do make such decisions for one reason or another and leave their homeland, if not renounce their citizenship, as a result of such decisions.

As for reasons why people decide to move across national borders, it is useful to distinguish between those people who are "pushed out" and those who are "pulled into". While some people are "pushed out" of a country for their views and acts which offend other people in that country, others are "pulled into" a new country for the benefits and rewards they expect to find in the host country. While some people are "pushed out" of a country because of discrimination, poverty and/or persecution, others are "pulled into" a new country for a better life there—culturally, economically, or politically.

Needless to say, it is not an easy task to distinguish among different reasons why people move from one country to another. In the case of "exiles", people are "pushed out" of a country, voluntarily in some cases, because of political oppression or power struggle. There are also cases where a large group of individuals are "pushed out" of a country because of their religious faith, or "pulled into" a new country in their search for a promised land. In general, the decisions to lead the life of exiles seem to be highly individual ones, with no official statistics being reported on this category of transnational migrants.

The term "refugees" used to refer to those people who are "pushed out" of their countries for political and cultural reasons and hence seek asylum in other countries to escape persecution at home. The United Nations' *Convention Relating to the Status of Refugees* signed in 1951 defines refugees as those people who are unwilling or unable to return to their country of origin "owing to a well-founded fear of being persecuted for reasons of race, religion, nationality, membership in a particular social group, or political opinion".

The UN Convention talks about what might be termed "political refugees", or "genuine asylum seekers". But many observers of the phenomenon of refugees today feel that this definition is too restrictive in the light of increasing numbers of people who seek asylum for "non-political" reasons. They therefore feel that it is necessary to add to the category of "political refugees" at least two other categories of "environmental refugees" and "economic refugees".

By "environmental refugees" is meant those people who are "pushed out" of their countries due to the damage done to the environment in these countries such as deforestation, soil erosion and water shortage. The phenomenon of "environmental refugees" started to be observed by development researchers in the 1970s. One report puts the total number of "environmental refugees" in the world as high as 10 million around 1985 (Jacobson [1989]).

The U.N. High Commissioner for Refugees, who keeps track of "political refugees", started to use the term "economic refugees", or "economic asylum seekers", in recent years to refer to increasing numbers of refugees who are "pushed out" of their home countries for lack of economic opportunities and hence seek better living conditions in other countries. Of the total of about 15 million refugees that the Commissioner estimated to be a reliable figure as of January 1991, over 80 percent were found in Africa, Asia and South America. This is no doubt a reflection of the political reality in these regions of the world which have poor records in upholding human rights. But it is also true that these are developing regions of the world, suggesting that these asylum seekers may well be trying to escape destitution and poverty in their home countries.

The economic pull of a better life beyond national borders has always been a strong motive for migration, as was indeed the case with the great wave of migrants from the Old World to the New World in the nineteenth century (Revenstein [1885]). But while migrants in the nineteenth century, especially those from Eastern Europe, often had to wait a few generations before they reached their final destination, transnational migration in today's interdependent world has become a relatively easy thing to do as national borders have been made increasingly porous by advances in transportation, communication and other technologies.

Whether transnational migration has gotten easier or more difficult, the nature of the economic disparities that separate developed from developing countries today would suggest the pattern of transnational labor migration to be almost a one-way traffic from the poorer regions of the world to the richer regions, i.e., from countries with lower standards of living to countries with higher standards of living. Although data on transnational migration is notoriously unreliable, somewhat limited empirical data on this subject seems to confirm this conjecture when disparities in standards of living are measured by levels of per capita GNP (OECD [1992]).

Needless to say, the level of per capita GNP is only one indicator of standard of living. To the extent that transnational migration is negentropic, the level of per capita energy consumption can also be used as a measure of standard of living (Taschdjian [1990]). But instead of focusing on any single factor, it seems more fruitful to discuss the pattern of transnational migration in terms of a variety of "push-out" and "pull-into" factors. Thus people are "pushed out" of their countries, in general, because of the lack of economic opportunities. Some sending countries actually consider the emigration of their workers to be a blessing in disguise because they can count on these workers' earnings abroad as a way of obtaining foreign exchange necessary for their economic development. People are also "pulled into" the receiving countries by the welcome mats extended by the people in these countries, including their friends and relatives. The receiving countries welcome the influx of foreign workers when they are willing to work at low wages in menial jobs. If these countries are suffering from a labor shortage problem, the availability of these foreign workers prevents the labor cost from going up, thus enabling them to retain their competitiveness in the global economy.

The Social Costs of Migration

At the rate at which the world's population is increasing today, the world expects to see its population increase by close to 100 million each year. The size of this increase, being significantly larger than the population of unified Germany, is certainly indicative of the magnitude of the burden population increase imposes on the world when we consider how many resources, real and financial, are needed if we are to guarantee a decent standard of living, if not the average standard of living enjoyed by the Germans.

For the world as a whole, population pressure serves as the Malthusian "limit to growth" and thus threatens to further increase the number of "environmental refugees" as the nations of the world—developed as well as developing—continue to exploit natural resources in their efforts to raise standards of living. Sooner or later, the world as a whole will have to share the social costs of over-population such as the accommodation of "environmental refugees", the loss of bio-diversity, and the acceleration of global warming.

The absolute size of the world's population is only part of the problem, however. The intractable nature of the population problem is that it is the developing part of the world that has a much faster rate of population growth. According to the United Nations' *World Economic Survey*, developing countries saw their population increase at 2.1 percent for the 1981-90 period while developed market economies at 0.6 percent. In order to maintain parity in standards of living, output in developing countries would have to grow at three times the rate of growth in developed market economies. The fact of the matter is that the growth rate of gross domestic output in developing countries was 3.0 percent as opposed to 2.4 percent in developed market economies for the 1981-87 period. It is thus clear that demographic trends perpetuate economic disparities between developed and developing countries. The migration of workers from developing to developed countries will continue as long as the disparity in the rates of population growth between these two groups of countries persists. Incentives for emigration are especially strong among young people, for over 80 percent of people between ages 15 and 25 are to be found in developing countries whose economies simply cannot provide enough job opportunities for them.

For individuals who manage to find their way into developed countries, their economic fortunes are expected to improve, regardless of whether they are skilled or unskilled workers. Some unskilled workers do very well indeed by finding employment in menial jobs shunned by young workers in developed countries who find more attractive job opportunities in service-oriented industries which better exploit their investment in human capital. Because of disparities in wage rates, migrant workers from developing countries manage to save a significant portion of their wages and send back monthly allowances to family members whom they have left behind. It is rare, however, that migrant workers are accorded the same privileges and rights as domestic workers in the receiving countries. As a result, they often face discrimination in terms of their access to unemployment compensation, health insurance and other social benefits.

There is a fundamental asymmetry between the country which sends out migrant workers and the country which accepts migrant workers. As a rule, the sending country benefits from the exodus of workers, except in the case of brain drain involving skilled workers, as it opens up job opportunities for other workers and relieves the country of the burden of supporting a large population. The receiving country on the other hand incurs a variety of costs as long as it is committed to guaranteeing the same privilege it accords to its citizens. Most of these costs are economic in nature, ranging from housing to training to health insurance costs. But there are also social costs in the sense that the influx of foreign workers threatens the cohesion of the receiving country as a social system by creating tension and friction between immigrant workers and local residents. In some cases, the tension and friction take an ugly turn in the form of a movement to expel foreign workers in order to assure the purity of the country's national culture, to protect jobs for domestic workers, or to maintain the sovereignty of the nation by eliminating potential intervention from the governments of the sending countries. This sort of phenomenon is already happening in such diverse countries as France, Germany, Japan, Italy, and the United States.

To the extent that the migration of people is from the poorer to the richer countries, transnational migration should serve as an equalizer in the distribution of income. But the persistence of the inequality of income distribution among nations of the world suggests that the movement of people alone is not sufficient to rectify the unequal distribution of income. For one thing, the remittances from migrant workers are too insignificant to affect the overall distribution of income, except for some nations such as Bangladesh and Egypt which get more than half of their export revenue from migrant workers' remittances. Then there is a matter of the difference that exists between developed and developing countries in the extent of investment in human capital. The difference is often such that those migrant workers who return to their countries of origin after a brief sojourn in foreign countries find their skills and knowledge they have acquired abroad to be of little use there. The fact that the returning workers' investment in human capital is not duly appreciated leads, in some cases, to the rejection of the values and life-styles of their home countries (Kubat [1984]).

But what is more important in thinking about the unequal nature of the global distribution of income is the relative mobility of people versus other things. If people are homogeneous everywhere in their abilities, inclinations and preferences and if goods and services are homogeneous in quality no matter where they are produced, the movement of goods and services will be sufficient to reduce, if not eliminate, inequalities in standards of living among nations. But the fact of the matter is that people are not homogeneous everywhere; people differ not only in their abilities, inclinations and preferences but also in their ethnic origins, the languages they speak and the value systems they subscribe to. And there is also a matter of training and maturation which we need to take into account when we talk of humans as economic resources. The upshot of all this is that the movement of people tends to be more cumbersome than the movement of goods and services and much slower than the movement of knowledge and information.

Policy Coordination in an Interdependent World

Incentives for transnational migration exist as long as there are differences among nations—culturally, economically, politically, or environmentally. And differences among nations will persist as long as human beings are more cumbersome than goods and services to move around and much slower than knowledge and information to be sent around. Of course, some dictators have tried, from time to time, to force arbitrary and willful migrations of people as if they were just things to be moved around. In general, the recognition that human beings are fundamentally different from other things seems to be at the root of policy debates on the problem of transnational migration. For example, should the countries of the world coordinate their migration policies so as to promote more equal distribution of income? If so, should policies be coordinated to encourage or discourage migration, given that things other than people can be substituted for the movement of people and that they, in fact, are much easier than people to be moved around?

The reality of the situation is that most countries impose restrictions of one sort or another on transnational migration. While no country enforces a policy of complete isolation, most countries restrict exits and impose quotas on the number of immigrants to be admitted. As is true with other political solutions, the quota policy tends to be applied arbitrarily—by lottery, for example—in allocating the number of limited entries among different nationality groups.

Another political solution would be to create a supra-national entity, as is the case with the European Community, to encourage the movement of people across national borders for economic reasons aside from the issue of citizenship. We can of course go a step further and devise an economic solution which treats citizenship as a commodity to be traded in an open, international market. If the migration of people is purely for economic reasons and if humans are to be treated mostly as economic resources, encouraging transnational migration this way may lead to an efficient allocation of human resources. It is unlikely, however, that this policy will lead to an equitable distribution of income worldwide because only those who can afford it will get to purchase the rights to citizenship of economically "desirable" countries.

If what is happening in the European Community is any indication, there is more to the issue of transnational migration than obtaining permission to move around. While transnational migration for economic reasons can be encouraged, there are cultural issues associated with national pride and cultural identity which tend to persist in the collective consciousness of a people. In other words, no policy coordination will be effective in an interdependent world unless it takes into account the implications of the fundamental conflict among culture, economy and polity as the subsystems of a social system at the global level. What is needed, therefore, is the willingness on the part of policy-makers to develop support systems which will encourage people to act as global citizens. This means, among other things, that people must be ready to carry many badges of citizenship, depending on whether they are acting as cultural beings, economic beings, or political beings. Indeed, what is wrong for a person to be French-speaking, work in an office in Germany, and carry Belgium citizenship?

Conclusion

The problem the transnational movement of people poses for an interdependent world is made intractable precisely because people are very different from other things which also move around the world. While goods and services can be shipped freely from one place to another and while knowledge and information can be spread quickly from one corner of the world to another, people as social creatures live with all their biological, cultural and political constraints that inhibit their free mobility. And as long as these constraints are there for the sake of maintaining social cohesion, it will be necessary to rely on the movement of things other than humans as a complementary means of achieving equality and justice among nations of the world.

The freedom of movement, in the sense of visiting places and seeking suitable employment, should be one of the basic human rights as it is indeed recognized as such in the United Nations' *Universal Declaration of Human Rights.* However, the policy of promoting transnational migration based on such a cultural ideal runs counter to the political realities of many countries which need to maintain social order and preserve an acceptable standard of living for their domestic residents. What type of policy coordination is needed regarding the problem of transnational migration depends, in the final analysis, on the degree to which the world is willing to perpetuate the social and economic disparities among nations in the face of the growing awareness that disparities of any form lead to the instability, and undermine the cohesion, of the world as a social system.

15. AUTONOMY, INTEGRATION AND IDENTITY: Can Political, Economic and Cultural Demands Made on Social Systems be Harmonized in the World of Global Interdependence?

Introduction

While a social system provides a framework to accommodate and realize diverse aspirations, desires and wishes of individuals, no social system can, by itself, satisfy all the aspirations, desires and wishes of all of its members. As a result, a social system is subject to tension and strain among its subsystems and its members at all times. The systemic tension and strain is especially acute among demand for political autonomy, demand for economic integration, and demand for cultural identity which needs to be eased if a social system is to provide a stable and viable environment for social life for its members.

The world of global interdependence presents a special challenge for social systems management because any social system is saturated with systems within itself as well as systems from outside that purport to accommodate these conflicting demands. This is the reason why we witness, at the same time, a tendency towards systems integration as represented by the European Community on the one hand and a tendency towards systems disintegration as represented by the break-up of the former Soviet Union on the other.

This chapter analyzes the realities of global interdependence in terms of the "global transactions matrix" which shows, in a matrix form, how a variety of systems within one social system interact vertically among themselves as well as horizontally with systems from other social systems in their political, economic and cultural transactions. While the matrix does not answer the question of what type of social systems configuration is optimal for organizing social life, it does offer insight into the nature of the conflicts and confrontations that develop among social systems in the world of global interdependence and can, therefore, be utilized in formulating policies to mediate these conflicts and confrontations.

The Global Transactions Matrix

What is characteristic of the nature of interaction among social systems in the world today is the degree to which a variety of systems and subsystems are involved in the network of transactions, from individuals to organizations, from local communities to regions, and from nation-states to transnational systems (Galtung [1980]). Moreover, the network of global transactions covers all areas of social life, from business to arts to sciences to ecology and the environment.

What type of global transactions a variety of social systems are involved in can be shown by developing the "global transactions matrix", expanding on a similar scheme employed by some researchers in international relations (Light & Groom [1985]). To be specific, the global transactions matrix records transactions between any two of a variety of systems and subsystems operating in the world of global interdependence by arranging these systems in the same hierarchical order both for "domestic" and "foreign" social systems.

Foreign Domestic	Transnational	National	Regional	Local	Individual
Transnational					
National					
Regional					
Local					
Individual					

It may be useful initially to classify the totality of global transactions into cultural, economic and political transactions, though in many cases it is difficult to characterize a specific transaction as purely cultural, economic or political. Take, for example, the case of an export of infant formula. This is an example of an economic transaction with cultural implications in that the use of infant formula suggests something about the life-styles and value systems of the societies involved in this transaction. The same is true of a cultural transaction, such as the exchange between two societies of two groups of performing artists, which obviously involves an "economic" exchange of money and resources.

What is more important than distinguishing among cultural, economic and political transactions in the global transactions matrix is to show the extent to which diverse systems from different societies are involved in any global transaction. This is so because global transactions encompass far more than "inter-national" transactions. For example, although international trade is conventionally treated as a transaction between nations and is recorded as such in official trade statistics, individuals and organizations are involved as workers, distributors, retailers and consumers as well as local communities whose public programs are affected by the success or failure of their business enterprises.

Diagnosing Conflicts and Confrontations among Social Systems

As the cultural, economic and political subsystems serve different demands of social systems for cultural identity, economic integration and political autonomy, it is rarely the case that any social system, by itself, is able to satisfy these different and often conflicting demands made on it (Koizumi & Koizumi [1992]). The task of coordinating among these conflicting demands is made more complicated in the world of global interdependence because no two social systems are engaged in purely cultural, economic or political transactions in isolation from other systems. Every society is involved in the network of complicated patterns of transactions with other societies in all areas of social life. As a result, the world of global interdependence is fraught with conflicts and confrontations—potential as well as real—among social systems and subsystems (Dahrendorf [1988]).

Consider the case of a trade friction between two nations, for example. To the extent that the friction is about the imbalance of trade between two nations, this is an example of a conflict between the two nations engaged in trade. But it is clear that individuals as consumers, organizations as labor unions and business firms, as well as local communities as providers of job opportunities and collectors of tax revenues are also stakeholders in the dispute. In dealing with a trade friction, therefore, it becomes necessary to carefully distinguish among global interests of the world system as a whole, national interests of the two nations involved, regional and local interests of the regions and local communities affected, and individual interests of workers and managers whose jobs are at stake. To this distinction among the hierarchy of social systems must be added a consideration of how much of the friction is economic and how much of it is non-economic. In a trade dispute over technologies, the cultural issue of what constitutes property rights is becoming a topic of hot debate between nations. Similarly, in the case of a trade dispute over agricultural products, the question of life-styles and value systems is also involved, in addition to the political issue of how crucial protecting farmers' interests is for the stability of the national government.

Foreign direct investment is another example where conflicts and confrontations develop between the parent corporation and the local community, between managers from the home country and employees in the host country. Conflicts and confrontations easily spill over into the cultural realm, especially when the home country and the host country represent different cultural traditions regarding such issues as decision-making style, the work ethic, and community services.

What is arguably the most explosive area where conflicts and confrontations abound in the world today is the area of ethnic rivalries and minority demands. The problem of ethnic rivalries and minority demands can, in some cases, be a political problem regarding fair representation in national politics, or it can be an economic problem concerning the equitable allocation of resources. It can also be a cultural problem reflecting the differences among groups of individuals as to their faith, language, and race. Social transactions between ethnic groups can be brutish and fierce as questions of justice, equity and identity are all at stake in any ethnic rivalry.

The problem of ethnic rivalries and minority demands acquires an insidious character in the world of global interdependence. Although the world is currently constituted politically as a system of sovereign nation-states, the nation-states do not necessarily constitute the best units for organizing cultural or economic life (Keohane & Nye [1972]). When an ethnic group is scattered in two neighboring nation-states, for example, the group is subject to two different political treatments, though it may culturally feel as forming one indivisible nation and may economically be influenced by the same forces of global capitalism.

All of these cultural and economic conflicts and confrontations are potentially present in the European Community as the Europeans try to promote economic integration to create a single market. While the member nations as well as the neighboring nations are fully aware of the potential economic benefits, this is a clear case where creating a transnational system does not automatically resolve conflicts among economic integration, cultural identity and political autonomy. The reason is that there is no single optimal unit of organizing social life which successfully resolves demand for political autonomy, demand for economic integration and demand for cultural identity.

Coordination and Harmonization

If conflicts and confrontations are unavoidable among social systems operating in the world of global interdependence, it becomes necessary to devise ways to relieve the tension and strain not only within a social system but also across social systems. Moreover, to the extent that the scope of transactions is truly global rather than international, national governments may not necessarily be the most effective units of resolving conflicts and confrontations among social systems even within a nation. Transnational systems can be more effective in certain types of transactions while truly global systems may be needed to resolve global conflicts and confrontations.

As things stand now, resolving trade friction is left up to negotiations between the two nations involved. However, if international trade is no longer a matter of trade between nations, more effective ways of resolving the friction may have to be developed including the involvement of a transnational organization such as the GATT, though this type of transnational system can find itself in a quagmire of competing national interests.

That economic conflicts and confrontations should be resolved at the transnational level is suggested by the fact that the logic of global capitalism constantly pushes towards integration of economic activities as a way of achieving efficiency and promoting growth. Transnational corporations, as agents of global capitalism, exert enormous influences today not only on the conduct of economic life but also on the conduct of social life in general. To the extent that these are transnational corporations, regulation of their activities must be made at the transnational level if it is to be effective. For example, in the area of environmental regulations, a mechanism for the global enforcement of responsible behavior towards the natural environment will have to be developed.

While the problem of ethnic rivalry is a national problem in some cases, it has become a global problem today not necessarily because ethnic groups are scattered in many nations but mostly because people have become increasingly aware of the presence and the impact of ethnic problems worldwide with their ready access to the news about ethnic conflicts and racial confrontations taking place in every corner of the world. Consequently, many systems and subsystems are already involved in resolving conflicts and confrontations from a global system such as the United Nations to national governments.

If the nature of a racial problem is mainly economic regarding the low status of minority groups within a nation, the national government may be the most effective unit of dealing with the problem with its redistributive policy. However, a racial problem of a global nature requires the intervention of a transnational organization. At the moment, the United Nations comes closest to such a transnational organization and is engaged in efforts to resolve conflicts and confrontations among ethnic groups. At the same time, many national governments are also involved in intervention in ethnic and racial conflicts taking place elsewhere in the world on account of their national interests or their humanitarian concerns.

The fact that many systems are involved in the task of resolving conflicts and confrontations among social systems and subsystems naturally raises an important question of what kind of system is most effective in resolving what type of conflicts and confrontations. While the United Nations is an outstanding example of a transnational system devoted to the task of resolving conflicts and confrontations at the global level, it is still a far cry from a truly global system equipped to deal with global issues. For one thing, the United Nations is an outgrowth of nineteenth-century political philosophy where nation-states were regarded as the most effective units of organizing social life. As such, there are some areas of social life where the intervention of the United Nations runs counter to the principle of sovereignty and self-determination as applied to nation-states. Moreover, the United Nations lacks the enforcing power of a national government in resolving national issues such as the military power to expel aggression or the legal power to appeal to the principle of eminent domain in protecting the environment.

Conclusion

There is no guarantee that the world of global interdependence will lead to the world of integrated social life. In fact, conflicts among demand for political autonomy, demand for economic integration and demand for cultural identity are being played out in the global stage today. There is no reason to expect, therefore, that the realities of global interdependence will automatically lead to the development of truly transnational systems to resolve global issues. But at the least we need to keep abreast of the ever-changing network of global interdependence. The global transactions matrix gives us a handle on identifying what levels of social systems are involved in what types of global transactions.

What sort of policies do we need if conflicts and confrontations in the world of global interdependence are to be resolved, if not eliminated? The common practice up to this point has been to appeal to the mediation of a third party which is supposed to be neutral with regard to the issues being contended. In the world of global interdependence, however, there is no such thing as a purely neutral third party on any issue. This means that the "third party principle" must be replaced by what might be termed the "superimposition principle". That is to say, to resolve a conflict between social systems, we need to superimpose a minimal system that envelops the conflicting interests of the systems in question. To choose an appropriate system that satisfies the "superimposition principle" is a precondition before the law of "requisite variety" is applied, which is concerned with the issue of the effectiveness of policies implemented (Ashby [1956]). To resolve a regional dispute, therefore, it is necessary to superimpose a national system, provided that the dispute does not have global implications. Needless to say, to the extent that most of our social transactions are global transactions, the "superimposition principle" points to the necessity of developing a truly global social system.

PART SIX

CULTIVATING GLOBAL AWARENESS

---

16. SYMBOLS, SIGNS AND SYSTEMS: Communication and Coordination in an Interdependent World

Introduction

Symbols, signs and systems are the devices we create and exploit for the purpose of facilitating communication and coordination in our social life. Although there are certain differences among them as to the mode of representation, the scope of communication and the effectiveness as the devices for coordination, symbols, signs and systems, when properly employed, all contribute to the cohesion of society as a system. If symbols, signs and systems are to facilitate communication and coordination, it is important that there exist common understanding among societal members as to what ideas they represent and what purposes they serve.

The problem of communication and coordination has become enormously complicated and, in some areas of social life, intractable as more and more societies with diverse historical traditions and cultural backgrounds have increasingly been brought into the network of global interdependence in recent years. If we are interested in the evolution of the world as a system, it is essential, therefore, that we examine the ways in which symbols, signs and systems serve as the devices for facilitating communication and coordination in social life. In fact, we must go a step further and examine the manner in which symbols, signs and systems need to be reorganized if they are to contribute to the cohesion of social systems interacting with one another in the world of global interdependence.

Examining the roles of symbols, signs and systems in social life is of utmost importance today because the world of global interdependence is fraught with conflicts and confrontations among different social groups within a nation and among different societies (Dahrendorf [1988]). Examining the nature of these conflicts and confrontations reveals that they reflect our failure to resolve the fundamental conflict among culture, economy and polity as subsystems of a social system which is interacting with other social systems in an interdependent world. Developing ideas for resolving this conflict deserves imminent attention of systems scientists.

The Ecology of Symbols, Signs and Systems

The world is full of symbols, signs and systems. Indeed, human history can be seen as a history of how we humans have gone about creating and exploiting symbols, signs and systems as the devices for facilitating communication and coordination in social life. We surround ourselves with pictures, letters, numbers and other devices which we create and exploit to represent our ideas, to communicate our intentions and to coordinate our actions.

Symbols are used to represent things as well as ideas and feelings. Representation can be abstract as in the case of mathematical symbols, specific as in the case of Chinese ideograms, and vague—even incomprehensible, except to the creator—as in the case of works of art. As is especially the case with works of art, symbols are employed because they offer a useful, non-linguistic mode of representing our ideas and feelings which defy exact translation into words (Jung [1969]). Since there are generally no social constraints or conventions as to what symbols should be used to represent what things, ideas and feelings, symbols are not normally employed as devices for mobilizing social action, except when the flag of a nation, for example, is used to elicit patriotic sentiment and action in times of international conflict.

Signs are more explicit in their social role as devices for communicating messages and coordinating actions. For example, road signs are explicitly intended to guide our actions—to maintain a certain speed, to stop, to prohibit entry into a one-way street, and so on. Signs are also used as trade marks to facilitate our association of products with their producers. Some signs are used as indicators of the state of a system and, therefore, play important roles in guiding the actions of policy-makers. Thus, the gross national product (GNP) and other macroeconomic aggregates are adopted as useful signs about the performance of the economy.

Systems are ubiquitous as they reflect our basic propensity to seek order and meaning in the world around us (Bertalanffy [1968]). The solar system conceived as a system tells us where in the universe our life as a species unfolds. The alphabet, as a system consisting of letters as elements, gives us a writing system as well as a system to organize our thoughts and actions (Logan [1986]). More importantly, we exploit systems as social contrivance to coordinate our actions. The legal system is an obvious example of this type of social usage of systems. So is the international trading system like the General Agreement on Tariffs and Trade (GATT), which serves to guide the behavior of nations as responsible members of the world economy.

The reason why systems are useful for social life is because a system, by definition, embodies our conception of unity and order among the elements which comprise it. Once a system is created in our social life, we are introducing rules and regulations by which our actions are restrained and coordinated. In fact, developing systems is our way of maintaining the coherence of society as a system.

However, conflicts and confrontations are inevitable because systems we create, as human inventions, are not free from defects and contradictions.

Representation, Communication and Coordination

There are differences as well as certain commonalities among symbols, signs and systems. Symbols, while useful as the medium for expressing our feelings and rich in their meaning because of their appeal to our intuition, suffer from ambiguity as the carrier of information and message. Signs, on the other hand, can be standardized and their meaning can be made uniform for members of the same society or, for that matter, for members in different societies. This process, the globalization of signs, is already taking place in many areas of our social life, reflecting the need to facilitate communication and coordination in the world of global interdependence. Systems, in a way, belong to a different logical type, for a collection of symbols, or signs, is itself a system. However, systems of one kind or another coexist with unorganized collections of symbols and signs as devices for communication and coordination in social life.

It is important to note, in this connection, that the same thing can at the same time serve as a symbol, a sign and a system. For example, the clock serves as a symbol for precision and a mechanistic outlook on life, a sign which tells us time of day, and a system which synchronizes and coordinates our social life (Landes [1983]). Money constitutes another example—and an important one at that because it is in the forefront of the globalization of our social life today. Money serves as a symbol of individual salvation for some, of social power for others, and of national pride for still others. But money, as the medium of exchange, serves as a sign which denotes the exchange value of a good or a service. And money starts to function as a system once it is widely accepted as the common medium of exchange. That is, once a single currency is adopted as the national currency, a national economy comes into being as a system and its behavior becomes subject to management by the monetary authority.

The fact that the same thing, like money, can at the same time serve as a symbol, a sign and a system has an important implication for the cohesion of a social system. While what money stands for may differ from one individual to another and from one society to another, money serves as a communicative device when it is used as the medium of exchange (Cornelis [1990]). To the extent that all participants are aware of the exchange values of things which money represents and adjust their actions as producers and consumers accordingly, money serves to coordinate actions in the production and distribution of goods and services. The economy is thus a system of social actions mediated by the use of money. Once a specific currency is adopted, money also becomes a device for controlling economic life. The Federal Reserve System, as the central bank of the United States, is indeed a "system" that facilitates and regulates economic life of Americans—and people in other nations as well in today's interdependent world economy.

Understanding how the same thing can at the same time serve as a symbol, a sign and a system is important because going from symbols to signs to systems as devices for facilitating communication and coordination in social life reflects, in a sense, the degree of social development. There is definite gain in the degree of precision in communication and coordination as symbols are replaced by signs, and signs by systems. The effectiveness of symbols and signs as devices for communication and coordination is limited by the degree to which they are accepted as the common carrier of specific information and message. When symbols and signs are converted into a system, they are converted into an integrative device that contributes to the cohesion of a social system.

Communication and Coordination in an Interdependent World

What is currently going on in the European Community (EC) serves to illustrate this point about the relationship between the use of symbols, signs and systems and the degree of social development. Here we have a system consisting of 12 member nations, currently engaged in a joint effort to develop a unified social system.

Even focusing on the economic aspect of unification, the European Community raises a number of difficult issues regarding system reform and transformation. For one thing, the twelve nations are not uniform in their degrees of economic development. For another, they do not share the same economic philosophy, especially as regards the appropriate degree of government involvement in the economy and priorities in macroeconomic policy-making. These differences not only translate themselves into differences in the mode of conduct of macroeconomic policy but are also embodied as differences in institutions of business and government. This is one reason why the effort to develop a common monetary system is still met with strong resistance.

Despite this and other resistances, the 279 directives originally outlined in the Project 1992 have been steadly adopted by the EC's Council of Ministers. However, adoption at the Council is no guarantee of observance by the member nations. Many of these directives still exist on paper only as the member nations have been reluctant and slow to rewrite national laws and regulations.

If unifying economic life is contentious, unifying cultural life is expected to be filled with conflicts and contradictions. Remember that these 12 nations are divided by the use of nine official languages. Just as with money, language is also a symbol, a sign, and a system. However, unifying languages is more complicated than unifying currencies because the use of language is deeply rooted in biology as well as psychology. Some language, like English, may emerge as the common language of business and diplomacy as it is already happening to some extent. However, we need to pay attention to the issue of ethnic and national identities associated with the use of language.

The unification of Europe offers an example which illustrates the difficulty we face in trying to overcome the fundamental conflict among culture, economy and polity as the subsystems of a social system. These subsystems, serving different human needs and being driven by different operational logics, sometimes complement one another but oppose one another at other times. Creating a supranational system which transcends systems that used to operate more or less autonomously is the necessary first step towards unification, whether that first step is taken in the realm of culture, economy or polity. In the case of EC, that first step was taken in the realm of economy.

The problem of unifying EC countries has been made enormously complicated by the dramatic events of 1989 which included the coming down of the Berlin Wall and the collapse of communist regimes in Eastern Europe. Some may argue that these events signify the convergence of two kinds of systems which used to divide Europe and the world into capitalist and socialist camps. Whether this convergence, or unification, in economic life will translate into unification in other areas of social life is still too early to predict, though there is every temptation to be caught up in the euphoria of the moment as the prospect of a new united Europe looms ahead.

Conclusion

The problem of promoting communication and coordination among diverse social systems enveloped in the world of global interdependence is made difficult because of the fundamental conflict among culture, economy and polity as the subsystems of a social system. Today culture, economy and polity oppose one another at the global level because the forces of globalization have not proceeded uniformly in the three realms of social life, with economic changes outpacing cultural and political changes.

The logic of the world economy aside which traps all nations of the world in the pursuit of material progress, the development of communications technologies has made it impossible for any nation to insulate itself from the forces of social change which no longer honor national boundaries. This is the reason why the Iron Curtain, which had long served as a symbol of division between two kinds of social systems, was torn down by the dramatic events of 1989. The tearing down of the Iron Curtain is only a symbolic event, however. The real task of integrating social life in two kinds of social systems is bound to encounter difficulties. Political expectations can be very easily frustrated unless real gains are quickly made in economic life as the picture of life on the other side of the fence exerts a powerful influence in the world linked by an extensive network of communications.

The world has become interdependent economically and is becoming increasingly so politically. Yet the world is still tragically divided culturally, as evidenced by daily reports of clashes and conflicts among different social groups and nations. If the conflict among culture, economy and polity is to be resolved at the global level, we must strive to develop a system within the context of the universal experience of individual human development which now takes place in the world of global interdependence. This suggests the strategic importance of education in cultivating an awareness of the roles which symbols, signs and systems play in facilitating communication and coordination in social life.

Systems scientists have a lot to contribute to this process of developing a system of global education which facilitates communication and coordination among diverse social systems now entangled in the complex web of global interdependence. At the same time, however, we systems scientists need constantly to remind ourselves of the tentative nature of the systems we create. Since systems are useful and powerful, there is every temptation on our part to cling to "our little systems" long after they have served their purpose, especially when our vested interests are at stake. After all, systems are as good as those who make use of them. This means that we need to internalize the systems that we create if they are to preserve the humaneness in us and to enhance the quality of human life. And we can only hope, with Lord Tennyson, that "our little systems have their day" before they cease to be as we go about our business of developing systems of this sort or that in our life as systems scientists.

Maybe?!

B'
Dave,

17. MANAGING GLOBAL INTERDEPENDENCE

Introduction

Deluged with news about terrorist attacks, ethnic riots, trade frictions, labor disputes, oil spills, acid rain, and the greenhouse effect, it is difficult to share Browning's optimism, "All's well with the world," even when "the year's at the spring and the day's at the morn." These and other stories which make the headlines in the morning news constantly remind us that we are living in an interdependent yet divisive world. While many of us now realize that the world is one ecologically and becoming increasingly so economically, we are painfully aware at the same time that the world is still hopelessly divided by conflicts and confrontations culturally and politically.

Divisive forces in the cultural and the political arena are sometimes so obstinate and persistent that many seriously question whether the world can ever be properly managed as a system. Indeed, we may well wonder whether we as a species, as some ethologists suggest (Lorenz [1966], for example), are prone to fits of violence because of our fate as an incomplete product of evolution. Perhaps we are prone to catastrophe because human history is ruled by the iron law of the conservation of catastrophe, as one historian has suggested (McNeill [1989]). Whether these observations are correct or not, it is important that we address ourselves to the challenge of managing the world as a system, especially when the expanded network of global interdependence quickly transforms a minor event taking place in a remote corner of the world into a major disturbance for the whole world.

If we are at all interested in managing the world as a system, the realities of global interdependence must be properly understood. This is so because so many of our actions and policies seem to be taken out of ignorance of and, in some cases, contempt for the facts of global interdependence, thus creating needs for further actions and policies to remedy the unforeseen and unintended consequences of our previous actions and policies.

The question of managing the world as a system is also a question of whether the human sciences which are employed to assist individuals and policy-makers today are adequately prepared to deal with the realities of global interdependence. Unless the realities of global interdependence are duly incorporated, the human sciences would not be able to contribute to the management of human affairs as they are expected to do.

The Nature of Global Interdependence

The network of global interdependence envelops us in every aspect of our social life. We are subject to ecological interdependence, in the ultimate sense, because we as a species are a product of evolution which has given rise to the natural world that constrains our existence as biological beings. However, the nature of our ecological interdependence has undergone important changes in recent decades as a result of the phenomenal increase in our capacity and propensity to influence, manipulate and transform the natural environment with our technologies.

Nothing better illustrates the extent to which we exert our influence on the environment than the recent controversy surrounding the greenhouse effect. Caused by the gases trapped in the lower atmosphere, the greenhouse effect is believed to be the culprit of the warming of our climate which has been steadily going on for the last century or so. The gases which contribute to this phenomenon such as carbon dioxide, nitrous oxide and chlorofluorocarbons(CFCs) are the byproduct of our economic activities—the burning of gas and oil to keep our factories running, the emission from our automobiles which we use to move about, and the production of goods and services which we engage in to improve our standard of living.

From our humble beginning as a fortuitous product of evolution, we have lately evolved ourselves into a major producer of evolutionary changes, transforming the environment with our ever-powerful technologies. Ecological interdependence is truly global as no individual or nation is immune from changes in the environment. Yet no individual, organization, community or nation is willing, or has the capacity, to manage the environment for the benefit of humankind.

That our economic activities can contribute to changes in the environment has disturbing implications. For example, most of the less developed countries (LDCs) of the world today are still under the spell of the conventional wisdom that industrialization is the key to economic development and improvement in standards of living. This has prompted countries such as Brazil, Indonesia, Thailand and the Philippines to destroy their tropical forests in order to make room for factories, plants and highways, thereby contributing to the increase in the global production of carbon dioxide in the atmosphere. LDCs are caught in a double bind in that, while they are desperately trying to catch up to the developed countries, they are increasingly under pressure to slow down the pace of deforestation of their tropical forests for environmental concerns which are more vocally raised in the developed countries.

LDCs are also handicapped by the need to operate in the world economy in which the rules of the game are largely dictated by a small number of developed nations in the core of the world system which are naturally interested in protecting and promoting their own national interests rather than those of a large number of developing nations in the periphery (Wallerstein [1974]). One of the important rules of the game which most nations subscribe to is the principle of free trade. The increase in international trade in recent decades, in which the proportion of the total product that goes into trade expanded from less than 10 percent in 1960 to over 30 percent by 1980, is testimony to a widespread adherence—voluntary or not—to this principle.

Far more dramatic than the increase in international trade has been the development of a world-wide network of financial transactions. As computers now make it possible to link financial centers scattered all over the world, it is not unusual to see over $900 billion of currencies being traded on a typical trading day across national boundaries as banks and other financial institutions scramble to take advantage of the slightest changes in exchange rates, interests rates and share prices. As a result, the world financial market has been transformed into an extremely fragile institution, in which a minor disturbance in one market can easily escalate itself into a major disruption of the world economy as was dramatically demonstrated by the stock market crash of 1987.

The migration of workers from the LDCs to the developed industrial nations represents a somewhat more complex phenomenon of global interdependence in that what is apparently an instance of economic interdependence has cultural as well as political implications. Nations such as England, France and Germany are experiencing the problem of "guest workers" from Third World nations as these workers have now established themselves as permanent residents with their own cultural traditions which are very different from those of their host nations. The presence of guest workers generates a network of cultural interdependence between their home countries and their adopted countries. The United States also faces the problem of migrant workers from its southern neighbors. Even Japan, which used to pride itself in the status of being racially a homogeneous nation, is experiencing the problem of migrant workers thanks to its newly acquired status as an economic superpower.

Needless to say, there are positive as well as negative sides to cultural interdependence. While learning about different cultures enriches our lives, cultural interdependence can very easily be turned into cultural conflicts and confrontations as culture, for most people, defines their identities as individuals as well as societal members. Violent conflicts and confrontations are not rare when cultural differences take the form of linguistic or religious differences. In fact, nations as diverse as Belgium, Canada, Ireland, India, Sri Lanka, Switzerland, and the United States share, to a greater or lesser extent, the problem of tensions and struggles originating in linguistic or religious differences among different groups of their citizens. Since linguistic or religious preferences are not constrained by national boundaries, cultural interdependence is also a global problem whose impact quickly spills over into the political arena, as is vividly evidenced by the spread of Islamic Fundamentalism. As the late Ayatollah Ruhollah Khomeini used to say, "Islam is political or it is nothing."

Ecological and economic interdependence can also lead to political interdependence. National governments are increasingly engaged in negotiations to work out the agreements to protect the common natural environment. They are also engaged in negotiations to remove tariffs and to establish the rules of international economic transactions.

Political interdependence is made complicated by the fact that nation-states are not the only powerful actors in world politics today. Just looking at the membership in the United Nations, the Non-Governmental Organizations (NGOs) far outnumber nation-states. Large NGOs, because they are transnational entities, can potentially exert wider influence over people living in different parts of the world than small nation-states. Large multinational corporations, for the same reason, exert their influence and affect people's lives in many parts of the world not only economically but also culturally and politically.

The nature of global interdependence in the world today is such that no problem is just cultural, economic, political or ecological. Every problem has all four aspects to it and, by virtue of complicated patterns of actions, reactions and repercussions, involves all nations of the world. For example, international trade, which involves the transfer of goods and services across national borders also involves the transfer of values and life-styles, as values and life-styles are invariably embodied in goods and services. Thus, economic interdependence that goes with international trade leads to cultural interdependence. International trade also leads to political interdependence as each nation tries to promote its own national interests which often conflict with those of other nations, and to ecological interdependence as the production of goods and services requires the extraction and transformation of natural resources in the environment.

Such are the realities of global interdependence which surround us in the world today. The world is indeed a complex system of connections and linkages among its constituent subsystems—individuals, groups, associations, organizations, and nations. A systems perspective is vital if we are to gain proper understanding of the complex realities of global interdependence.

Managing Global Interdependence

As the realities of global interdependence are complex, attempts which are being made to manage global interdependence do not seem to follow any systematic principles. Most of these attempts are more or less stopgap measures designed to address the issues at hand and are not based on any long-term analysis of the behavior of the world as an interdependent system.

In the area of the environment, rather remarkable events have taken place just in the last few years. The Montreal Protocol on ozone protection signed in 1987, the World Congress on the Changing Environment held in Toronto in June 1988, and the Earth Summit held in Rio de Janeiro in June 1992 are a few examples of an international endeavor to try to manage the effects of human activities on the environment. However, these agreements are not universal in scope either in terms of the kinds of emissions to be regulated or in terms of the number of nation-states involved. Even among the signatory nations, their effectiveness is bound to be limited as we lack a "decider" which regulates and oversees the behavior of nation-states in world affairs (Miller [1978]).

As a matter of fact, the traditionalist approach in world politics, which sees the world as consisting of autonomous political units called nation-states having sovereignty over their territories, is increasingly being made irrelevant by the realities of global interdependence. Even a large nation such as the United States no longer possesses the kind of autonomy and independence from foreign influences idealized in the writings of political philosophers, including the Framers of the U.S. Constitution, in the eighteenth century. As the world's largest debtor, the United States can no longer manage its own economy without the cooperation of such nations as Japan, Germany and the Great Britain.

Cooperation in macroeconomic policy-making may not be forthcoming willingly when an economic issue has a cultural overtone. This is obviously the case with the dispute between the United States and European nations regarding the liberalization of trade in agricultural products. It is also the case with the trade friction between the United States and Japan over the liberalization of markets for agricultural products. Although primarily viewed in the United States as an economic problem, liberalizing trade in agricultural products, as far as the Japanese government is concerned, means a threat to the political stability of that nation which is largely maintained by the support of farmers as well as to the cultural tradition of reciprocal human relationships nurtured in an agrarian community.

If the world is to be managed at all, it needs to be managed as a social system. This means that the world must be seen as a system consisting of the subsystems of culture, economy and polity which, though they complement one another, nevertheless conflict one another as they are systems which address themselves to rather different sets of issues in human affairs.

Culture, economy and polity conflict with one another because, for one thing, these subsets of human actions serve different "human needs". While economy tries to satisfy the material needs, culture covers the kinds of activities which are designed to meet the spiritual needs such as values, beliefs and identities. Finally, polity tries to meet the human need for order and security in social life.

Culture, economy and polity also conflict with one another because they represent different kinds of actions taking place in different "fields of action". With the exception of a society which is geographically isolated from all other societies, which is culturally homogeneous and which is economically self-sufficient, no society is expected to find a uniform field of action for culture, economy and polity. While the field of action for culture is dictated by such factors as language, religion and ethnic origin, the field of action for economy tends to overcome these factors as well as political constraints imposed by nation-states.

Culture, economy and polity further conflict with one another because they do not share the same "value system" in judging the efficacy of actions. While economy has a very clear-cut linear value system based on a simple notion that more is better than less, culture and polity do not share such a linear value system.

In fact, decision-making in the cultural and political arena is often inconsistent and haphazard.

The complex patterns of global interdependence in the world today indicate that conflicts among culture, economy and polity are not confined by national boundaries. There are simply too many cultural and economic institutions and organizations in the world today which escape the sovereignty of nation-states. The situation can be interpreted as an instance of the "type-R" dysfunction in the world system (Koizumi [1988]). In fact, the nation-state, though still powerful and important, is just one agent of social change in the world today. Non-governmental organizations and multinational corporations have become too numerous and powerful to be constrained by the sovereignty of nation-states. If the units of cultural and economic life are becoming increasingly global, it is clear that the units of political life must also be made global.

One way in which the globalization of political life can be accomplished is to develop the United Nations into a "head", a world-state if you will, rather than a "center" as it is today. Whether the world today is ready for this, there does not seem to be any other effective solution to the problem of managing global interdependence. After all, it is the role of polity to define a social framework within which different aspirations, commitments, and missions of different cultural groups and economic organizations are to be reconciled and coordinated. Universal acceptance of the *Universal Declaration of Human Rights* is perhaps the first necessary step which all nations can take today towards realizing this political goal.

Conclusion

The human sciences, judging from the way they are practiced today, do not seem to be equipped to deal with the complex realities of global interdependence. For one thing, most human sciences still operate within the Cartesian paradigm which views reality space as consisting of the sum of non-interacting parts. As such, they cannot deal with the realities of global interdependence which exist among different subsystems of a social system. Nor, for that matter, can they deal with the fact that each one of these subsystems cannot be characterized as either purely cultural, purely economic or purely political. Today each organization is at the same time a cultural, an economic and a political entity and operates in the context of eco-systemic interaction with other organizations.

Whether, as Wordsworth once pondered, "the world is too much with us," there is no question that the world needs to be managed if it is to serve as a hospitable place for human growth and development. Ultimately, the blame for mismanagement must be placed on each one of us who is supposed to embody the spirit of, and behave as, a citizen of the world. What is lacking, then, is the kind of self-knowledge that helps us define our identity in this interdependent world. Of course, as Goethe aptly pointed out, "man knows himself as much as he knows the world." If ignorance of the world of global interdependence is at the root of today's problems, then we must redress the balance in school curriculum, as one anthropologist suggested (Montagu [1966]), by placing the fourth "R" at the top of our priority in education. For, in the world of global interdependence, the individual exists only in the context of social relationships with other individuals.

18. THREE R'S OF GLOBAL EDUCATION

Introduction

The image of education as a disciplined and often boring life of learning basic skills has long been with us as typified by such lines as Shakespeare's "whining schoolboy, with his satchel and shining morning face, creeping like snail unwilling to school" (*As You Like It*) and Blake's "Under a cruel eye outworn, the little ones spend the day, in sighing and dismay" (*Songs of Innocence*). Boring as it may have been, there is no denying the fact that modern education has contributed to the raising of standards of living for people living in the industrial part of the world with the teaching of the three R's of reading, writing and arithmetic (Cipolla [1969]).

On the other hand, modern education has long been criticized by humanists and social scientists for its universal emphasis on utilitarian values. Education, they argue, has become an institution which selects and trains individuals to meet the needs of society instead of providing an environment for each individual to cultivate his own unique potential.

The debate between two schools of thought regarding the goal of education, i.e., whether education ought to respond to the needs of society or should focus on cultivating the individual's potential as a human being, is as old as the history of thought. On the one hand, we find such illustrious thinkers as Plato, Augustine, Aquinas, and Montaigne advocating the idea that education ought to be a vehicle for cultivating the human potential. On the other hand, we find equally illustrious names such as Aristotle, J.S. Mill, Rousseau, and Adam Smith supporting the idea that education ought to aim for the training of socially productive citizens.

As in all matters of consequence in human affairs, the wisdom of the golden mean suggests that the truth lies somewhere in between and, therefore, that both aspects of education are necessary for both the individual and society. After all, education is administered on individuals who exist as societal members. The only new perspective we need to add to this old debate is an explicit recognition of the fact that the space of individual existence has expanded to cover the whole world as the society in which he learns and grows up is enveloped in the network of global interdependence. This means that the question of what education entails must also be examined in the context of the world of global interdependence.

Why Global Education?

Whether education caters to the promotion of societal needs or to the cultivation of individual potential, there is little doubt that education today must be "global" education. This is so because the phenomena of global interdependence are the facts of social life for all societies of the world and, as such, need to be incorporated into the content as well as the method of education.

Culturally, no individual is immune from news about the life of other people in other parts of the world thanks to the development of communications technologies. Economically, every individual has a chance of working for a domestic firm which is engaged in international trade or a firm owned and managed by foreign nationals. Politically, no government can fully exercise autonomy and self-determination because of the pressures exerted by foreign governments and/or international organizations. In short, the web of global interdependence covers every aspect of our social life today, irrespective of where our social activities take place. As a result, every individual, whether he realizes or not, is engaged in "global transactions" in his daily life.

Studying the phenomena of global interdependence must therefore be the primary mission of global education, for the world is indeed an interdependent system among individuals, groups, associations, organizations, and nations. And studying the phenomena of global interdependence means learning about the manner in which individual existence, regardless of where it takes place, is enveloped in a web of global interdependence with these systems. What is needed, in other words, is education founded on a systems view of man in which man is seen as an open system whose existence is defined in the space of interaction with other open systems such as other individuals, groups, communities, organizations, and nations (Bertalanffy [1981]).

Conventional education leaves much to be desired when it comes to dealing with the phenomena of global interdependence. The nominalist view still dominates in social discourse in that society is seen, more or less, as the sum of individuals and the world as the sum of nation-states. The way traditional academic disciplines organize and present knowledge of the world around us reinforces the nominalist conception of society and the world in that little effort is made to teach how bits of knowledge obtained in different disciplines are related to one another and can therefore be transcended into a unified view of what the world is like. It is obvious that both the content and the method of conventional education need to be reformed if the phenomena of global interdependence are to be accepted as the facts of social life in the world today.

This is not to deny that the globalization of education is being pursued here and there. There are many schools which call themselves international schools and cater to students from many nations, with some efforts being made to incorporate the teaching of languages and cultures into the core curriculum. There are also multinational schools which, with their branch campuses scattered in different parts of the world, export the curriculum developed in the home country.

These are actually examples of the globalization of educational institutions rather than of education itself. For the globalization of education, both the content and the mode of education must be globalized.

Three R's of Global Education

If the globalization of education is what is needed, how can that be accomplished? What are the basics that need to be incorporated into global education? We propose three R's of "relations", "reciprocity", and "responsibility" to replace three R's of traditional education—"reading", "writing" and "arithmetic".

"Relations" are what ought to be discussed, studied and taught in global education. Relations are essential because they are what the systems view of the world is all about. According to the systems view, the world is seen as consisting of systems, where systems are, by definition, relations among component elements.

In the first place, our social life evolves around human relations. Man as an open system is born into relations with family members and grows up in the space of evolving relations with family and other societal members around him. By suggesting the importance of human relations in social life here, we are not suggesting that these human relations are to be treated as a fixed set of relations which constrain individual autonomy, which is often the case with the "Five Relations" of Confucius as they have been practiced in some societies with the Confucian tradition. Human relations are of evolving nature because they are defined in the space of human development.

Needless to say, relations in the world which define man as an open system are not limited to human relations. There are also relations among groups, organizations, and nations. Relations can also be found among the world's languages and cultures as well. And our relations with the natural environment are becoming of critical importance as we humans as a species have come to exert an increasing influence on the natural process and phenomena. All of these relations form the realities of our existence in the world of global interdependence. Learning about all these relations in the world of global interdependence is also a matter of formulating answers to the perpetual questions of life for us humans: what we are, how we have got to be where we are, and where we are going.

All relations in the world of global interdependence are "reciprocal" relations, for "reciprocity" is what global interdependence is all about. It goes without saying, however, that the meaning as well as the extent of reciprocity differ from one relation to another. While in some cases "reciprocity" means direct bilateral relations between two things, it may mean indirect linkages through a number of intermediate relations in others. In any event, to the extent that interdependence is a fact of life, "reciprocity" must constitute the second R of global education (Becker [1986]).

Individuals do not exist independently of other individuals as they, as open systems, need to exchange matter, energy and information with other individuals.

The meaning of individual autonomy, therefore, needs to be carefully reinterpreted. Individual autonomy in the world of global interdependence must mean that an individual exercises a certain degree of control over his space of human development in his life as a biological being, a psychological being, and a social being.

It is to be noted that "reciprocity" also characterizes the mode of global education. In traditional education we tend to put too much emphasis on the learners as the sole recipients of the benefits of education, for education is seen as a one-way communication of the facts of the world. However, even in the conventional setting of classroom teaching, those who teach also receive benefits and satisfaction as partners of the students' human development. In fact, there is a growing body of evidence showing that the effectiveness of education is enhanced by incorporating "interaction and feedback", i.e., by incorporating "reciprocity" whether the learner's interaction is with humans or with machines.

The same can also be said about what is normally characterized as a hierarchical relationship among individuals in organizations and societies. When organizations and societies are seen as systems, the principle of "reciprocity" is always at work in that the actions of those who are commanded also influence those who command in the network of actions, reactions and repercussions.

Relations in the world of global interdependence imply "responsibility" on the part of all individuals and other subsystems of the world. In the first place, as citizens of the world we owe it to ourselves to learn about relations which define the conditions of our existence in the world. The fact that the world we live in is the world of global interdependence means that we also owe it to our fellow human beings, for our actions, whether we realize it or not, are connected to actions of other individuals by a complicated web of actions, reactions and repercussions. Finally, we owe it to our future generations to behave responsibly. As is especially the case with our relationship with the natural environment, what is required is what Hardin termed "mutual coercion" of responsible behavior to avoid the tragedy of the commons (Hardin [1968]). Responsible behavior means a certain degree of self-restraint, for we owe it to future generations to leave the benefits that nature has conferred on us as a species.

Three R's of Global Education and Traditional Disciplines

Man as an open system exists in the space of interaction with other open systems. This space in which human development takes place can be conveniently divided into the biological, the social and the psychological space corresponding to man's "relations" to nature, to his fellow human beings and to his inner self (Koizumi [1990]). Classifying all relations man faces in his development into these three groups is useful for pedagogical reasons in that it establishes linkages with various academic disciplines which are being taught in a rather fragmented manner in traditional education.

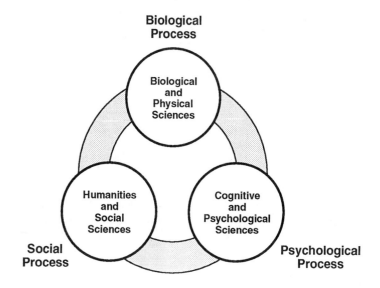

The biological aspect of human development takes place in the space of man's interaction with the natural environment, i.e., the space in which man as a biological being interacts with other living systems and matter. Thus all of the natural sciences are relevant in exploring the nature of relations in this space—astronomy, biology, chemistry, geology, meteorology, physics and so on. The social aspect of human development defines the space of man's interaction with other human beings. Thus all of the social sciences—anthropology, communication, economics, political science, sociology and so on—become relevant as they are concerned with exploring the nature of human relations in social settings. In addition to the social sciences, the traditional disciplines of humanities such as history, literature and philosophy are also relevant. Finally, the psychological aspect of human development is the inner space within man's psyche in which ego and self interact. Thus all of the cognitive sciences including physiology, psychoanalysis, psychology, and the science of artificial intelligence become relevant as they give us insight into the nature of relations we form in our own mental world. To these scientific disciplines must be added humanities such as literature and philosophy as they also provide valuable insight into our inner world.

It is important for global education to explicitly recognize the connections and linkages among humanities and sciences. Unless such connections and linkages are explicitly recognized and efforts are made to incorporate them into the curriculum, global education ends up inheriting one of the troublesome dilemmas of traditional education called "overspecialization" (Rudloff [1988]). Global education is necessarily a transdisciplinary education in that it aims to explore the nature of global interdependence in the world around us.

Global education is also a transcultural education in that the space of human development defined above is not culture-specific but is universally applicable. In fact, the framework defined here can be used for the learning of cultures by examining how different cultures go about explaining what the relations in the three spaces ought to be. This point is important because in the world of global interdependence an educational philosophy based on an ethnocentric notion that only one culture ought to be the subject as well as the medium of education must be rejected. By the same token, the so-called "multiculturalism" must also be rejected, for the universal acceptance of that philosophy would lead to a multicultural world without any prospect of cross-fertilization. Without cross-fertilization, there would be no societal learning. Indeed, "societal learning" must be an integral part of global education if the world of global interdependence is to function as a viable and stable system.

Conclusion

The three R's of traditional education do not qualify as the three R's of global education because they represent the basic skills to be acquired if individuals are to become productive citizens of the industrial society. The industrial society, while it is still to be realized in many parts of the world, has given way or about to give way to the information society in some parts of the world. Indeed, there is no reason why modernization and economic development should always imply transition from the agricultural to the industrial to the information society. The world as a system is an eco-system of all kinds of societies with different stages of development and different ideas as to how modernization and economic development ought to proceed.

The three R's of global education—relations, reciprocity and responsibility—do not suggest a specific manner in which social life is to be organized. They are the basics of education regardless of the type of society and independent of the degree of social development, to the extent that every social system exists in the space of eco-systemic interaction with other social systems. And every individual experiences life, as he goes through various stages of human development, in the space of interaction with other individuals, groups, associations, organizations, nations, and nature. It is this systems view of the world as the space of global interdependence that suggests "relations", "reciprocity" and "responsibility" to be the three R's of education.

Learning the three R's of global education should not be a disciplined and boring experience. In fact, there is no reason why global education should be confined to classroom education. The three R's of global education can be taught and learned in any setting where reciprocal relations are to be found. Since reciprocal relations are everywhere to be found, global education must necessarily be an "open" education. Indeed, for those who aspire to learn about the world of global interdependence, the world is the classroom. To paraphrase Shakespeare, "All the world's a [classroom] and all the men and women merely [learners]."

BIBLIOGRAPHY

Armstrong, J.A. *Nations Before Nationalism*. Chapel Hill: University of North Carolina Press, 1982.

Arnold, Matthew. *Culture and Anarchy: An Essay in Political and Social Criticism*. New York: Macmillan, 1924.

Ashby, W. Ross. *An Introduction to Cybernetics*. London: Chapman and Hall, 1956.

Bateson, Gregory. *Mind and Nature: A Necessary Unity*. New York: Dutton, 1979.

Baumol, William J., and W.G. Bowen. *Performing Arts—The Economic Dilemma*. New York: The Twentieth Century Fund, 1966.

Becker, Lawrence. *Reciprocity*. Chicago: University of Chicago Press, 1986

Bell, Daniel. *Cultural Contradictions of Capitalism*. New York: Basic Books, 1976.

Bendix, N. *Nation-Building and Citizenship*. New York: John Wiley & Sons, 1964.

Bertalanffy, Ludwig von. *General System Theory*. New York: George Braziller, 1968.

_____. *A Systems View of Man*. Boulder: Westview Press, 1981.

Boulding, Kenneth E. "An Evolutionary Interpretation of History". *Ecodynamics*. Beverly Hills: Sage Publications, 1978.

Braudel, Fernand. "Will Capitalism Survive?" *The Wilson Quarterly*. Spring 1980, 108-116.

_____. *The Structure of Everyday Life*. New York: Harper and Row, 1981.

Brix, V.H. "Politics through Macroscope". *News Letter*. Cybernetics Academy Odobleja, 10, 1986, 21-23.

Bronfenbrenner, Urie. *The Ecology of Human Development*. Cambridge: Harvard University Press, 1979.

Cannon, W.B. *Wisdom of the Body*. New York: Norton, 1939.

Capra, Fritjof. *The Turning Point: Science, Society, and the Rising Culture*. New York: Simon and Schuster, 1982.

Carr, E.F. *What is History?* Harmondsworth: Penguin, 1964.

Cipolla, C.M. *Literacy and Development in the West*. Harmondsworth: Penguin Books, 1969.

Cohen, R. *The New Helots: Migrants in the International Division of Labor*. Aldershot: Avebury, 1987.

Cornelis, Arnold. "Can Society Be Conceived As A Communication System?" Koizumi, Tetsunori, and George E. Lasker, eds. *Advances in Education and Human Development*. Windsor: International Institute for Advanced Studies in Systems Research and Cybernetics, 1990, 85-89.

Crozier, Michael, Samuel P. Huntington and Joji Watanuki. *The Crisis of Democracy*. New York: New York University Press, 1975.

Dahrendorf, Ralf. *The Modern Social Conflict*. London: Wedenfeld and Nicolson, 1988.

Dahl, Robert A. *Dilemmas of Pluralist Democracy: Autonomy vs. Control*. New Haven: Yale University Press, 1982.

Darwin, Charles. *The Origin of Species*. New York: Hill and Wang, 1979.

Descartes, Rene. "Discourse on the Method of Rightly Conducting the Reason". *Great Books of the Western World*. London: Encyclopaedia Britannica, 1952.

Dogen. "Body and Mind". Tsunoda, R., W.T. de Bary and D. Keene, eds. *Sources of Japanese Tradition*. New York: Columbia University Press, 1958.

_____. "Realizing the Solution". Tsunoda, R, W.T. de Bary and D. Keene, eds. *Sources of Japanese Tradition*. New York: Columbia University Press, 1958.

Downs, Anthony. *An Economic Theory of Democracy*. New York: Harper and Row, 1959.

Einstein, Albert. *Relativity: The Special and General Theory*. New York: Crown, 1916.

Eisenstadt, S.N., and R. Lemarchand, eds. *Political Clientelism, Patronage and Development*. Beverly Hills: Sage, 1981.

Eliot, T.S. "Burnt Norton". *Four Quartets*. New York: Harcourt Brace and World, 1971.

Ellul, Jacques. *The Technological Society*. New York: Alfred A. Knopf, 1964.

Erikson, Erik H. *Childhood and Society*. New York: Norton, 1950.

_____. *Young Man Luther*. New York: Norton, 1958.

Exupery, A.S. *The Little Prince*. New York: Harcourt Brace Jovanovich, 1971.

Fodor, J.A. *The Language of Thought*. New York: Thomas Y. Crowell, 1975.

Freud, Sigmund. *Totem and Taboo*. London: Hogarth, 1913.

_____. *Civilization and Its Discontents*. London: Hogarth, 1930.

_____. *Five Lectures on Psycho-Analysis*. New York: Norton, 1977.

Galtung, Johan. *The True Worlds*. New York: Free Press, 1980.

Gardner, Howard. *The Mind's New Science*. New York: Basic Books, 1985.

Gödel, Kurt. *On Formally Undecidable Propositions*. New York: Basic Books, 1962.

Habermas, Jurgen. "History and Evolution". *Telos*. 39, Spring 1979, 5-44.

Hall, Edward J. *Beyond Culture*. Garden City: Doubleday Press, 1976.

Hankiss, Elemer. "In Search of a Paradigm". *Daedalus*. Winter 1990, 183-214.

Hardin, Garrett. "The Tragedy of the Commons". *Science*. 162, 13 December, 1968, 1243-1248.

Havel, Vaclav. "A Conversation with President Havel". *World Press Review*. March 1992, 14-16.

Heilbroner, Robert L. "Do Machines Make History?" *Technology and Culture*. 8, July 1967, 335-345.

Heisenberg, Werner. *Physics and Reality*. New York: Harper and Row, 1958.

Hobsbawn, E.J. *Nations and Nationalism since 1780: Programme, Myth, Reality*. Cambridge: Cambridge University Press, 1990.

Homans, G.C. *The Human Group*. London: Routledge and Kegan Paul, 1951.

Huxley, Thomas. *Evolution and Ethics*. Oxford: Oxford University Press, 1893.

Inkels, Alex. "Linking the Whole Human Race: The World as a Communications System". Sawyer, Herbert L., ed. *Business in the Contemporary World*. Lanham: University Press of America, 1988, 133-163.

Jacobson, Jodi L. "Abandoning Homelands". *State of the World 1989*. Washington: World Watch Institute, 1989.

James, Harold. *A German Identity, 1770-1990*. New York: Routledge and Kegan Paul, 1990.

James, William. *The Varieties of Religious Experience*. New York: New American Library, 1958.

Jaynes, Julian. *The Origin of Consciousness in the Breakdown of the Bicameral Mind*. Harmondsworth: Penguin Books, 1980.

Jung, Carl G. *The Structure and Dynamics of the Psyche*. Princeton: Princeton University Press, 1969.

_____. *The Archetypes of the Collective Unconscious*. Princeton: Princeton University Press, 1969.

Kennedy, Paul. *The Rise and Fall of the Great Powers*. New York: Random House, 1987.

Keohane, Robert, and Joseph Nye. *Transnational Relations and World Politics*. Cambridge: Harvard University Press, 1972.

_____. *Power and Interdependence*. Boston: Little Brown, 1977.

Keynes, John M. *The General Theory of Employment, Interest and Money*. London: Macmillan, 1936.

Koizumi, Hisako, and Tetsunori Koizumi. "Specialization, Socialization and Identity in an Interdependent World". *Systems Research.* 8(3), 1992, 35-41.

Koizumi, Tetsunori. "Knowledge, Power and Democracy". *Cybernetica.* 31(3), 1988, 215-224.

_____. "The Mode of Theorizing and the Nature of Knowledge: A Systems Approach to Learning and Knowledge Acquisition". Koizumi, Tetsunori, and George E. Lasker, eds. *Advances in Education and Human Development.* Windsor: International Institute for Advanced Studies in Systems Research and Cybernetics, 1990, 1-13.

Kubat, D., ed. *The Politics of Return: International Return Migration in Europe.* New York: Center for Migration Studies, 1984.

Kuhn, Thomas S. *The Structure of Scientific Revolutions.* Chicago: University of Chicago Press, 1970.

Landes, D.S. *Revolution in Time: Clocks and the Making of the Modern World.* Cambridge: Belknap, 1983.

Lao Tsu. *Tao Te Ching.* New York: Vantage Books, 1972.

Levy, M.J. *Modernization and the Structure of Societies.* Princeton: Princeton University Press, 1966.

Light, M., and A.J.R. Groom. *International Relations: A Handbook of Current Theory.* London: Francis Pinter, 1985.

Logan, Robert K. *The Alphabet Effect.* New York: William Morrow, 1986.

Lorenz, Konrad. *On Aggression.* New York: Harcourt, Brace and World, 1966.

_____. *Behind the Mirror: A Search for a Natural History of Human Knowledge.* New York: Harcourt Brace Jovanovich, 1977.

Maruyama, Magoroh. "Morphogenesis and Morphostasis". *Methodos.* 1961, 251-296.

Maslow, Abraham. *Motivation and Personality.* New York: Harper and Row, 1970.

McNeill, William H. "Control and Catastrophe in Human Affairs". *Daedalus.* Winter 1989, 1-12.

Merton, Robert K. *Social Theory and Social Structure.* Glencoe: Free Press, 1957.

Miller, James. *Living Systems.* New York: McGraw-Hill, 1978.

Minsky, Marvin. *The Society of Mind.* New York: Simon and Schuster, 1985.

Montagu, Ashley. *On Being Human.* New York: Hawthorn Books, 1966.

Mumford, Lewis. *Technics and Civilization.* New York: Harcourt, Brace and World, 1963.

Needham, Joseph. *The Grand Titration: Science and Society in East and West.* London: George Allen and Unwin, 1969.

OECD. *Trends in International Migration*. Paris: Organization for Economic Cooperation and Development, 1992

Parsons, Talcott. "Evolutionary Universals in Society". Parsons, Talcott, ed. *Sociological Theory and Modern Society*. New York: Free Press, 1967, 490-520.

Parsons, Talcott, and A. Shils, eds. *Towards a General Theory of Action*. Cambridge: Harvard University Press, 1952.

Pedover, Saul K., ed. *Thomas Jefferson on Democracy*. New York: New American Library, 1939.

Piaget, Jean. *The Construction of Reality in the Child*. New York: Basic Books, 1954.

_____. *Genetic Epistemology*. New York: Columbia University Press, 1970.

Polanyi, Karl. *The Great Transformation*. Boston: Beacon Press, 1957.

_____. *The Livelihood of Man*. New York: Academic Press, 1977.

Polanyi, Michael. *The Tacit Dimension*. New York: Doubleday, 1966.

Popper, Karl. *Quantum Theory and the Schism in Physics*. Totowa: Rowan and Littlefield, 1982.

Putnam, Hirary. *Mind, Language and Reality: Philosophical Papers*. Cambridge: Cambridge University Press, 1975.

Revenstein, E.G. "The Laws of Migration". *Journal of the Royal Statistical Society*. 48, 1885, 167-227.

Rossiter, Clinton, ed. *The Federalist Papers*. New York: New American Library, 1961.

Rousseau, Jean Jacques. *The Social Contract*. Harmondsworth: Penguin Books, 1968.

Rudloff, W.K. "Proposal for a Systems Approach to Universal Education". Lasker, George E., ed. *Advances in Systems Research and Cybernetics*. Windsor: International Institute for Advanced Studies in Systems Research and Cybernetics, 1988, 234-239.

Russell, Bertrand. *Power: The Role of Man's Will to Power in the World's Economic and Political Affairs*. New York: Norton, 1938.

_____. *Freedom versus Organization, 1814-1914: The Pattern of Political Change in 19th Century European History*. New York: Norton, 1962.

Schopflin, G. "The Political Tradition of Eastern Europe". *Daedalus*. Winter 1990, 55-90.

Schumpeter, Joseph A. *The Theory of Economic Development*. Cambridge: Harvard University Press, 1949.

Simon, Herbert A. *Models of Bounded Rationality*. Cambridge: MIT Press, 1982.

Smith, Adam. *The Wealth of Nations.* New York: Modern Library, 1937.

Spengler, Oswald. *The Decline of the West.* New York: Knopf, 1928.

Sperry, Roger. *Science and Moral Priority.* New York: Columbia University Press, 1983.

Staub, Hans O. "The Tyranny of Minorities". *Daedalus.* Summer 1980, 159-168.

Tai, Hung-Chao, ed. *Confucianism and Economic Development: An Oriental Alternative?* Washington: Washington Institute Press, 1989.

Taschdjian, Edgar. "Phase Transitions in Social Systems". Koizumi, Tetsunori, and George E. Lasker, eds. *Advances in Education and Human Development.* Windsor: International Institute for Advanced Studies in Systems Research and Cybernetics, 1990, 109-114.

Tawney, R.H. *Religion and the Rise of Capitalism.* London: John Murray, 1926.

Taylor, Frederick W. *The Principles and Methods of Scientific Management.* New York: Harper and Brothers, 1911.

Thom, Rene. *Structural Stability and Morphogenesis.* Reading: Benjamin, 1975.

Toffler, Alvin. *The Third Wave.* New York: William Morrow and Co., 1980.

Toynbee, Arnold. *A Study of History.* London: Oxford University Press, 1954.

Unger, Roberto M. *Knowledge and Politics.* New York: The Free Press, 1975.

Vendryes, Pierre. "Truth and the Science of Man". *News Letter.* Cybernetic Academy Odobleja, 14, 1987, 7-19.

Waits, C.R., W.S. Hendon, and H. Horowitz, eds. *Governments and Culture.* Akron: Association for Cultural Economics, 1985.

Wallerstein, Immanuel. *The Modern World System.* New York: Academic Press, 1974.

Weber, Max. *The Protestant Ethic and the Spirit of Capitalism.* London: Allen and Unwin, 1930.

_____ . *Economy and Society.* Berkeley: University of California Press, 1978.

White Jr., Lynn. "The Historical Roots of Our Ecological Crisis". *Science.* 155, 10 March 1967, 1203-1207.

Wiener, Norbert. *Cybernetics, Or Control and Communication in the Animal and the Machine.* Cambridge: MIT Press, 1948.

Wordsworth, William. *Poetical Works.* Oxford: Oxford University Press, 1936.

Zeami. "On the Mind Linking All Powers", "The Book of the Way of the Highest Flower", "The Nine Stages of No in Order". R. Tsunoda, W.T. de Bary, and D. Keene, eds. *Sources of Japanese Tradition.* New York: Columbia University Press, 1958.

SOURCE NOTES

All of the articles included in this book have been presented at conferences, forums and symposia in the last several years and most have subsequently been published in journals, proceedings, and edited books. *SOURCE NOTES* here contain exact references to these journals, proceedings, and edited books. For the purpose of maintaining coherence and unity among the articles included in this book, these articles have been revised slightly from their originally published versions. They are reprinted here with the permission of the original publishers.

Chapter 1 – Adapted from "The Mode of Theorizing and the Nature of Knowledge: A Systems Approach to Learning and Knowledge Acquisition". Koizumi, Tetsunori, and George E. Lasker, eds. *Advances in Education and Human Development*. Windsor: International Institute for Advanced Studies in Systems Research and Cybernetics, 1990, 1-13.

Chapter 2 – Adapted from "The Importance of Being Stationary: Zen, Relativity and the Aesthetics of No-Action" by T. Koizumi. In *Mind and Body: East Meets West (pp. 61-68)* by S. Kleinman (Ed.), 1986. Champaign, Illinois: Human Kinetics. Copyright 1986 by Human Kinetics Publishers, Inc. Adapted by permission.

Chapter 3 – Adapted from "Mind, Consciousness and Knowledge: East and West". Lasker, George E., Tetsunori Koizumi, and Jens Pohl, eds. *Advances in Human Systems and Information Technologies*. Windsor: International Institute for Advanced Studies in Systems Research and Cybernetics, 1992, 1-6.

Chapter 4 – Adapted from "Human Autonomy and Social Cohesion". *Analyse de Systemes*. March 1989, 69-73. Adapted and reprinted by courtesy of the review *Analyse de Systemes*.

Chapter 5 – Adapted from "Culture and the Social Order". Hendon, William S., Harry Hillman-Chartrand, and Harold Horowitz, eds. *Paying for the Arts*. Akron: Association for Cultural Economics, 1987, 175-183.

Chapter 6 – Adapted from "Knowledge, Power and Democracy". *Cybernetica*. 31(3), 1988, 215-224. Adapted and reprinted with the authorization of the International Association for Cybernetics.

Chapter 7 – Adapted from "Economic Development as a Cybernetic Process". Koizumi, Tetsunori, and George E. Lasker, eds. *Advances in Education* *and Human Development.* Windsor: International Institute for Advanced Studies in Systems Research and Cybernetics, 1990, 103-108.

Chapter 8 – Adapted from "Coordinating Social and Technological Development". Lasker, George E., ed. *Advances in Systems Research and Cybernetics.* Windsor: International Institute for Advanced Studies in Systems Research and Cybernetics, 1989, 1-7.

Chapter 9 – Adapted from "Nationalism as Ideology, Nationalism as Emotion, and the Pitfalls of National Development". Trappl, Robert, ed. *Cybernetics and Systems Research.* Singapore: World Scientific, 1992, 1193-1199.

Chapter 10 – Adapted from "Cultural Diffusion, Economic Integration and the Sovereignty of the Nation-State". Sack, Peter, Carl P. Wellman, and Mitsukuni Yasaki, eds., *Monismus oder Pluralismus der Rechtskulturen? Rechstheorie.* Berlin: Duncker and Humblot, 12, 1991, 313-319.

Chapter 11 – Adapted from "Global Interdependence and the Patterns of Interaction and Transformation of Human Systems". Presented at the *13th International Congress on Cybernetics*, 1992. Adapted and published with the authorization of the International Association for Cybernetics.

Chapter 12 – Adapted from "History as a Systems Science". Lasker, George E., Tetsunori Koizumi, and Jens Pohl, eds. *Advances in Human Systems and Information Technologies.* Windsor: International Institute for Advanced Studies in Systems Research and Cybernetics, 1992, 113-120.

Chapter 13 – Adapted from "Global Interdependence and the Ecology of Social Ethics". *The Proceedings of the 12th International Congress of Cybernetics.* Namur, Belgium: International Association for Cybernetics, 1990, 603-608. Adapted and reprinted with the authorization of the International Association for Cybernetics.

Chapter 14 – Adapted from "Exiles, Migrants, Refugees: The Nature and Implications of the Movement of People in the World of Global Interdependence". Presented at the *Sixth International Conference on Systems Research, Informatics and Cybernetics*, 1992. Adapted and published with the authorization of the International Institute for Advanced Studies in Systems Research and Cybernetics.

Chapter 15 – Adapted from "Autonomy, Integration and Identity: Can Political, Economic and Cultural Demands Made on Social Systems be Harmonized in the World of Global Interdependence?" Presented at the *Sixth International Conference on Systems Research, Informatics and Cybernetics,* 1992. Adapted and published with the authorization of the International Institute for Advanced Studies in Systems Research and Cybernetics.

Chapter 16 – Adapted from "Symbols, Signs, Systems: Communication and Coordination in an Interdependent World". Lasker, George E., Tetsunori Koizumi, and Jens Pohl, eds. *Advances in Information Systems Research*. Windsor: International Institute for Advanced Studies in Systems Research and Cybernetics, 1991, 32-37.

Chapter 17 – Adapted from "Managing Global Interdependence". Lasker, George E., and Robbin R. Hough, eds. *Advances in Support Systems Research*. Windsor: International Institute for Advanced Studies in Systems Research and Cybernetics, 1990, 1-5.

Chapter 18 – Adapted from "Three R's of Global Education". Lasker, George E., Tetsunori Koizumi, and Jens Pohl, eds. *Advances in Information Systems Research*. Windsor: International Institute for Advanced Studies in Systems Research and Cybernetics, 1991, 528-532.

NAME INDEX

SUBJECT INDEX

ABOUT THE AUTHOR

Tetsunori Koizumi teaches economics at The Ohio State University, Columbus, Ohio. He has a Ph.D. in economics from Brown University. He is a fellow of the International Institute for Advanced Studies in Systems Research and Cybernetics. He is the co-editor, with George E. Lasker, of *Advances in Education and Human Development*, 1990. Among his articles are "Economics as a Study of Man" and "The Oriental Ideal in Art and the Art of Economic Man in the Orient".